WHAT COULD POSSIBLY GO WRONG?!?

HOW TO GO FROM COMPLETELY CLUELESS TO TOTALLY PREPARED

DEDICATION

First, and foremost, I want to dedicate this book to Jesus Christ my Lord and Savior. If not for God's hand in orchestrating who I am today I would be just another lost sheep; both spiritually and in life.

To my husband, my soulmate, and fellow farmhand, who has encouraged me in every step of my preparedness-journey.

To my Twitter #PrepperTalk Pals who have stuck by me all these many years and help make the hash tag both an international success, and synonymous with all-things-preparedness; thank you from the bottom of my heart.

And, to all the women who now "get-it" and have traded in their heels for hills, and to those who are just awakening. Remember ... we're all in this together!

FORWARD

Before my journey into preparedness, I pretty much lived a life in total ignorance and avoidance about what was going on around me. No politics. No current events. No world affairs. Instead, I chose to live in a world of no newspapers or news; avoiding anything that even remotely hinted at negativity or ugliness. In fact, the closest thing to news I came was watching *Good Morning America* on television each morning as I readied myself to go to work – mostly for the entertainment value, and having little to do with wanting to know more about what was happening in the world around me. For me, news was a lot of heartache and just way too depressing for my neat and orderly little world.

My husband and I both worked in the corporate world; me at a large prestigious company in downtown; and my husband; a television producer, and former advertising executive, had his office at one of the top entertainment meccas in the country. We worked hard and collectively our incomes gave us the gated community life-style with all the fun toys, vehicles, and great vacation spots.

My days were filled with work and client meetings, lunches, after hour mingling and, eating out at some of the best restaurants in town. I mean, why dirty the kitchen for just two people, right? So, no cooking for me! At night, I continued my love of socializing by jumping on the internet to see who was doing what on all the social media networks I was involved in. On the weekends I would go treasuring hunting (to garage sales) with my sister – which meant seeking out even more *things* to purchase. I was a consumer at its best.

Surprisingly for some, my husband is a prepper (or survivalist depending on who you ask), and was way before the phrase was even coined. As such, he always made sure we had ample food stored (that did not need refrigeration), and a way to cook the food (and boil water) using an outdoor grill or camping stove should the electrical power go out. There was also plenty of water to drink, bathe, cook, and clean with. He even had emergency bags packed and ready to go – for what I was never really sure of, and frankly didn't care to know. I just chalked his ways up to being a boy scout in his youth and, "always wanting to be prepared" – whatever that meant. I was way too busy focusing on more important matters like the latest trends in clothes, handbags and shoes, or flipping through my ever-growing stacks of fashion magazines and, socializing with my friends and family, for me to be the least bit concerned with anything else that was going on around me. Disasters; or the possibility of disasters, were the farthest thing from my mind. Sure, I helped board up the windows of our house during hurricane season, but then that's what everyone in Florida did – after all we lived in the hurricane capital of the world. But, beyond that, prepping was my husband's *hobby* - not mine. After all, what could possibly go wrong?

At some point however, I began to notice an increase in the street traffic in our beautifully manicured gated-community. Doing a little research (some may call it *snooping* … whatever), I learned that some, of what I *thought* were wealthy neighbors with their nice clothes, expensive vehicles and all-things-money, were suddenly renting their homes out to anyone who could pay the hefty monthly mortgage payments; to avoid foreclosure – even if it meant renting to multiple families under one roof., all as the result of the housing market bubble bursting. Thankfully my husband and I could pay our mortgage – so how could this bubble bursting possibly affect us?

As time went on though, with more and more people "moving-in" to our community, we began to see a rise in crime – something that was almost nonexistent in the past. It was not uncommon two and three nights a week to hear the roar of a sheriff's helicopter circling overhead with its huge spotlight panning back and forth, illuminating the neighborhood, in search of the latest bad guy, a break in, physical assault, or theft. I was insistent that our home have the latest security system, including glass breaking sensors and motion detectors – oh and lights on every corner of the house outside with a strobe-light effect that would flash if anyone got near the house. After all, I wanted to be safe in my own home.

Then the stock market crash, again this was something I knew little to nothing about. Finance, other than finding a great deal shopping was another topic I totally steered clear of. For me the stock market was just a way to a means for my retirement. It wasn't until I looked at one of my statements for my 401k; something I had paid into for years but never bothered to pay attention to, that I got the shock of my life! My account balance was dwindling, and fast! I was losing almost seven thousand dollars a month and had not even realized it! Like I said, that was money that I had planned to live in the same lifestyle I had become accustom to when we retire. To catch up, I would have to work another lifetime to recoup all of that money! I decided right then and there, I would march into the human resources department at my office (the company I worked for was self-insured so they handled all the financial investments too), and tell them I wanted to take my money out *now* before it was all gone! Unfortunately, it didn't quite work out the way I had played it out in my mind. The HR director informed me that the money could only be withdrawn in one of two ways; upon my death or if I quit my employment with the company. I just couldn't understand it, this was my money! I should be able to do with it as I please!

My little world somehow was getting darker and darker, but I was determined to keep up the same optimistic disposition I had always had, no matter how bad it got around me. And, one particular afternoon I was feeling just this way. I had left work a little early; around 4:30 pm, on a beautiful sunny afternoon. A lot of people were already out on the sidewalks winding their way between one another to get to their destinations, as the traffic began to build in anticipation of rush hour. As I exited the parking garage waiting for an opening in traffic to pull out, I noticed two men running at full pace down the sidewalk towards me. I had a split second decision to make – crossover over the sidewalk so I could ease into traffic which would make the men have to run around behind my car, or wait until they passed in front of my car and then pull out. "What if they were running to catch a bus?" I thought to myself. If they ran behind my car it might cause them to miss their bus. So, I decided to wait. I would sit tight allowing them to continue running down the sidewalk. What happened next can only be described as surreal. As I sat waiting for the men to pass; watching people and traffic go back and forth, I heard the door handles on both the front and back passenger doors being pulled on. I looked over to see these same two men I was waiting to cross in front of me now trying to get into my car! Fortunately for me, I had the doors locked; this time, but that didn't seem to deter them in the least bit. With expletives spewing from their mouths, guns in hand, they were violently banging on the car windows, demanding that I unlock the doors and let them in. This was all happening in broad daylight with people crowding the sidewalks and traffic all around. Thankfully, someone had notified the police and within minutes, officers with guns drawn, surrounded my car and apprehended the bad guys. I later learned that these men had robbed someone at gunpoint at an ATM and were looking for a get-away vehicle. Mine.

After the attempted carjacking, shaken, I finally understood that the world I thought I lived in was not the real world at all. Bad things happen to good people too. I began to ask questions and research how I could better prepare myself for anything that may come my way in the future. I didn't want to find myself vulnerable again by not knowing what was going on around me. Preparedness is arming you with knowledge and skills to deal with any sort of disaster - from the loss of a job or revenue-contributing spouse, to a natural or man-made disaster, it makes no difference. You plan for one and you can plan for them all.

This book is about thinking of what could go wrong and planning for these events – with or without prior notice, which you may not otherwise had planned for. I have purposely created NOTE sections in the book, for you to write things down to help you plan too.

As you now know, I was once like the majority of consumer loving people in our country. In fact, I was probably just like you. But I made a conscious decision that

I would not be a victim. I decided to take control of my life and my destiny. And, now I will share what I have learned along the way in hopes that you too can prepare. After all, what could possibly go wrong?

CONTENTS

Band-Aids and Beans and Bullets - "Oh My"   46

What If Tomorrow a Disaster Really Did   50
Happen?: Preparing Today for Tomorrow

Words Can't Describe It: Visualizing a Disaster   54

I Think I Can – I Think I Can: Mental   57
Preparedness

Life Is A Stage: Practicing for Your Survival   61

What's So Golden About A Golden Horde?   65

What A Great Personality: Knowing You   68
Disaster Personality

Get Your Head Outta the Sand People!: How To   72
Share Awareness About Disasters

3   **SELF-DEFENSE**   **76**

Hey Gimme That!: When What You Have Is   77
Taken

Cutting Off Sound: Situation Awareness   82

When People Do Unspeakable Things: And   85
They Will

What Weapon?: When Your Firearm Is Taken   88
Away From You

Got A Dollar?: Cheap Home Security Ideas   91

❧ 1 ❧
Disasters Come
In All Sizes

Disasters Look a Lot Different Up-Close: Surviving a Life-Threatening Disaster

If you were to ask a person or people who have survived a catastrophic disaster; natural or man-made, they would most likely tell you nothing was the way they would have imagined it would be. "Why?" you ask. Well simply because most of us have only seen disasters through a keyhole image on a television set or in pictorials of a magazine or book. It doesn't matter how big your television screen is, or how brilliant the photographs are, the images can never capture the true catastrophic event as it truly is up close and personal - the sounds or lack of, the smells and the debris, all take on a sort of surreal-ness about them.

Growing up in Florida I have seen my share of catastrophes and disasters. From massive sinkholes to the destruction caused by hurricanes Andrew, Charlie, Frances and Ivan, and the Space Shuttle *Challenger* disaster. But one catastrophe stands out from all the rest; one I will never forget, as its images are burned into my memory. It was March 31, 1972, a beautiful spring day. I was in the bathroom of our family's small cinder block home; washing my hair in the sink when all of a sudden I heard an unusually loud plane go overhead. Now, a plane flying over our house was nothing to cause alarm; in fact it was an every day and night occurrence. Located right in the flight path of McCoy Air Force Base; home to the Strategic Air Command (SAC) 306 Bombardment Wing, and B-52 bombers – the longest lived front-line military aircraft - was our home.

With planes flying overhead at all hours of the day and night, you just kinda got used to hearing that certain roar they made, and most times could actually tune them out – well at least enough to sleep at night. But on this particular day, what was odd about this plane was the noise the engines were making – it was different this time. Flying overhead was a huge, eight-engine B-52 Bomber with a fuel load of about 44,000 gallons, with one engine on fire and multiple engine failures.

From what I have come to learn, the bomber was attempting to make it back to the runway after its take-off, but fell short on the approach; it was too high and to the left. The bomber hovered for a second, then rolled to the side and went directly into the ground … and our neighborhood.

I remember feeling the rumble of the tremendous explosion; it seemed like every ounce of fuel went up in a split second, sounding like a huge bomb going off and blanketing a two-block housing area with intense heat. Through the eyes of a child; to me it resembled the classic nuclear mushroom we have all seen in pictures and on television as the plane hit the ground carving a 150-foot crater in the field where it slammed.

Thankfully, our home was a block away and facing the crash site. As I looked out the window in horror I could see the flames from the wreckage mirrored in the windows of our house and those of neighboring homes across the street; all making it seem as though the entire neighborhood was on fire.

I grabbed a bath towel and quickly wrapped my hair up in it as I ran out the front door. I can still remember how the intense heat felt on my face from the blazing inferno and the overwhelming smell of burning fuel in my nostrils.

I made it to the crash site before the fire department or Air Force first responders arrived. The neighborhood looked like a war zone – or what I perceived as a war zone at my young age. There was wreckage scattered everywhere – with no real aircraft remaining to speak of – that is, other than the landing gear which ended up in the middle of someone's living room, and the tail section; where sadly the only recognizable body of a crew man was found.

Military olive-green aircraft pieces of all sizes were everywhere. And ... a lot of fires, car fires, house fires, trees on fire, fences on fire, and burning fuel.

Within hours, with smoke still smoldering, little yellow flags began to spring up – markers where human body *parts* were found.

As far as my little eyes could see there were yellow flags on bushes, in the streets, in trees; everywhere. No bodies, just body parts and flags of the deceased crewmen. Seven B-52 crew members died instantly that day, and one 10-year old boy died three days later from his burns. Eight other people on the ground were severely injured with burns as well.

As tragic and surreal as this event was to a little girl, it has always amazed me – even to this day - why more people weren't injured or killed on that horrific day. After all, it was Good Friday; a holiday ... and all schools were out.

What You Can Do To Prepare

Until you have experienced a catastrophic event up close and personal, you really have no idea what you will encounter. The whole landscape of an accident and/or

4

disaster scene will take on an entirely different look and feel. Objects that were once whole suddenly turn into a bazillion different sizes, and indistinguishable bits and pieces. Odd odors permeate the air.

We've all probably witnessed or happened upon an automobile accident at some point in our life. It's hard to fathom a vehicle reduced to a tangled heap of twisted metal, with parts strewn everywhere. Black streaks crisscross the road where the vehicle attempted to avoid another or brake at the last minute; signs, guardrails, and fencing bent and twisted – the stench of gasoline and oil permeating the air. And there lying in the roadway or in the crushed vehicle are the white-sheet draped bodies of the deceased; once a happy family on their vacation. It's hard to imagine that life could be taken so suddenly. Think how a house that has been hit by a tornado can instantly be reduced to nothing more than pieces of tattered fabric, glass and wood shards and, mangled metal all piled next to a slab of concrete foundation, once someone's happy home.

A simple slip on an icy surface can result in a fracture to the leg with protruding bone fragments or, a cut from slicing vegetables can end with exposed tendons and ligaments. No matter what the event, nothing, and I mean nothing, can prepare you for what a disaster will look like or even what you've imagined it will look like. You need to mentally prepare yourself for sights, sounds, and smells never before experienced. - Just sayin'.

Pandemics:
Yes It Can Happen Here

I used to think pandemics only happened in other countries. I mean, we live in the United States of America, right? And as the Star Spangled Banner so eloquently puts it … "'O'er the land of the *freeeeeee* …" To me, land of the free meant free from all the un-pleasantness you read about in those other countries, you know, sickness, droughts, hunger, disease? My way of thinking was this; our country has all these fancy laboratories and pharmaceuticals companies so we surely were the land of the germs free too.

Then April 2009 rolled around. One morning I awoke to the newspaper headlines … "Outbreak of Swine Flu in Mexico." Reading the article, I was so thankful I lived in a *germ-free* country unlike these other countries. I didn't have a pig. And, I didn't live near a farm or zoo. I mean, the article was talking about pigs after all, – okay swine, so I was safe. Or so I thought.

Updates continued daily on the swine flu, with reports of the Mexican government closing down most of their public and private offices as they tried to contain the spread of the virus, dishing out surgical masks and hand-sanitizer gel like they were lollipops at a bank teller's window.

Now, flash forward two months, by June 2009, the swine flu had spread globally, – that's around the world! *The World Health Organization* (WHO) (not The Who – the English rock band of the 60s) declared the outbreak a pandemic and changed the name of the virus from swine flu to the H1N1 virus, so scientific, huh? Maybe like me,

6

others thought they wouldn't get the virus because they weren't around pigs? But, *gulp* ... a pandemic in our country?

Out of curiosity, okay maybe it was sheer fear, I looked up the word pandemic. The definition, read in part: "... *an epidemic of infectious disease that spreads through human populations across a large region; for instance a continent, or even worldwide.*" *Gulp* number 2! "Is a worldwide pandemic even possible?!" I wondered. And the answer was yes.

By August 2009; four months after the first news hit about the H1N1 virus there was a worldwide pandemic; including the United States of America. The virus spread by human to human, through coughing or sneezing by those with the virus or by touching something with the virus on it, and then touching your mouth or nose. Therefore, everyone, and everything was suspect for having the virus.

Thankfully, by August 2010, a year to the date of being formally labelled a worldwide pandemic, the H1N1 virus was officially downgraded.

Then Ebola reared its ugly head. In 2014 the news hit of the first case of the Ebola virus on U.S soil. Many people were once again caught off-guard. As I had once believed, they thought of these viruses as only happening in other countries. Unfortunately with our transit system, trains, planes, buses, subway, ferries, ships and all the modes of transportation in between, we are sitting ducks for the next big pandemic.

So what can we do to protect ourselves in the future from the spread of contagions? Well *protect* is pretty subjective, but we can start practicing our protection by reminding people around us to cover their nose *and* mouth, and cough or sneeze into their sleeves or handkerchief, for starters (I know it congers up snotty sleeves for me too.)

Next, wash your hands often with soap and water, especially if you are around people who are coughing or sneezing or after *you* cough or sneeze. Oh, and, if you are using the sleeve method, you might want to take a moment and wipe off your sleeve as well (*gross* ... I know.)

Now to objects with the virus. As an *FYI*, touching the belongings of a sick co-worker, friend or family member, can make you sick as well if you touch your eyes, nose or mouth after handling anything of theirs that has the virus on it, so carry an alcohol-based hand sanitizer with you and use it often when you don't have access to soap and water. (A handkerchief is also a great way to open doors without using your hands.)

It's also a good ideal, to have disinfectants on hand and use them often on touched surfaces; which is anywhere there are people, bathrooms, kitchens, Snack-machines, restaurant tables, chairs, railings, doors handles, elevator buttons, doorknobs. Get the gist? Wipe down e-v-e-r-y-t-h-i-n-g. Some viruses can live on hard surfaces for several hours, up to a day. And, the infected person can infect others beginning one day before their symptoms start and up to seven or more days after becoming sick. That means that you could pass on the virus to someone else before you know you are even sick, as well as, while you are sick or vice versa.

Now, you may be saying to yourself, "I will just go and get some *Tamiflu* or *Relenza* from my doctor so I won't get sick." Unfortunately, you may not be able to get these medications because they are meant to *treat* the virus not *prevent* it. Also these medications have to be prescribed by a healthcare provider and without the virus you ain't gettin' it. Now add this to the equation, these medications are only effective in the first 24 hours of being infected. Most people don't even consider going to the doctor until two or three days into their illness.

What I have used with success with influenza, and also grow in my garden (you may want to consider this too) are elderberries. Black elderberry syrup can actually help boost your immune system and shorten the virus. To buy elderberry syrup in the store can cost upwards of $15 for a four ounce bottle – steep I know, that is why I grow my own elderberries, and boy are they high yielding!

For me, an ounce of prevention; or in the case of store-bought elderberry syrup, four ounces, is better than a pound of cure!

What You Can Do To Prepare

Germs are everywhere. Always have been always will be. Some are good germs, some are bad. However, with the ever-increasing number of people traveling abroad and/or coming into our country every day from other countries and, with the mass transit of buses, taxis, planes, railways, and subways, et cetera, there is a need for more awareness and vigilance of our surroundings and what is going on, around us. Ebola was a big scare for us all and resulted in a huge panic to the citizens of our nation and healthcare providers alike. We were not ready. None of us were ready.

With the next pandemic, yes I say next because it's only a matter of time before the next contagion rears its ugly head, be ahead of the game by having the basic needs of water and food already in place thereby taking some of the panic out of the equation. (Keep in mind you could be isolated for up to four-months.) If such a need does arise for you to stay in-doors and isolate yourself and family from the public; you will be okay, whether you are attempting to avoid a virus or recover from one.

Pandemics are not going to wait for you to do your grocery shopping and get your supplies in order. Consider having, for each member of your family, a Tyvek suit or hooded coveralls with elastic on the wrists and ankles (like painters wear), a pair of safety goggles (or swimming goggles), a box or two of N95, N99 or N100 respirator masks with the exhalation valve, a box of nitrite gloves (industrial grade) and antibacterial soap.

Another thing that most don't consider is that if you or a family member in your household has the virus, whoever it is, needs to be quarantined from the rest of the household, the same holds true of someone new coming into the household.

Remember that viruses can take upwards of three to 14 days to manifest themselves – if you will recall Ebola took 21. Have at a least 100 foot roll of clear plastic (four millimeters or more), to seal off a room or section of the house, and a couple rolls of duct tape to tape up the plastic, and to seal up the wrist and ankles of your coveralls.

The unknown is scary. Not being prepared for the unknown makes it even scarier. - Just sayin'.

Notes:

It's Not My Fault:
Nuclear Power Plants near U.S. Fault Lines

Japan is one of the most *earthquake ready* countries in the world, and yet when it was hit by a devastating 9.0 earthquake, and tsunami, on March 13th, 2011, causing a level seven nuclear meltdown at the Fukushima Daiichi Nuclear Power Plant, it resulted in an estimated $300 billion dollars in damage. Now when I say *earthquake ready*, I mean ready in the sense that Japan's buildings and structures were tested to withstand up to a 7.0 earthquake – and look what happened.

So what about the rest of us? What about the United States of America? How ready are *we* for an earthquake? What would happen if *we* were hit by a magnitude 9.0; or bigger? The largest earthquake recorded was 9.5 in 1960 in Valdivia, Chile.

Did you know that a large percentage of the states in our nation are at risk of a major earthquake? In fact, 39 out of the 50 states are in a moderate to high risk area for seismic activity. Sounds scary huh? Some of these fault lines, especially the ones that are on the surface of the earth, may seem obvious, but what about the others lying deep within the earth's crust obscured by a thick layer of soil? Is it out of sight, out of mind for most of us?

Let's take a closer look at our country's fault lines. There is the *New Madrid Fault*, which is one of the most vulnerable regions in the United States and would directly affect a range of states including Illinois, Missouri, Tennessee, and Indiana. The *Rampo Fault*, lies between the

Appalachian Mountains and the Piedmont areas and would have devastating effects on states like New York, New Jersey, and Pennsylvania. The *Ridgefield Fault* could result in severe damage to Connecticut, and the surrounding regions. The *Denali Fault* which crosses the state of Alaska and into Canada would affect Alaska and Canada. And, lastly the *San Andreas Fault*, which spans the state of California, from Cape Mendocino to the Mexican border. The *San Andreas Fault* is part of what is known as, the *Ring of Fire*, with other countries bordering Pacific Ocean.

Okay, now that we know where the fault lines are, let's turn our focus to the power plants in our nation. California has the *San Onofre Nuclear Generating Station* and the *Diablo Canyon Power Plant* and both are positioned near California's fault lines. Remember Japan's 2011 devastating earthquake, and the resulting nuclear radiation fall-out of their reactors? Notice I mention two stations in California? An earthquake near these reactors could result in a double whammy. Take the example of a magnitude 9.0 earthquake, and then couple this with the inevitable tsunami that will surely ensue. Toss in the Pacific winds and you have a crippled nation in less than an hour. Hundreds of thousands of people from California will attempt to flee to cities and states already overpopulated. The airborne nuclear fallout would spread like sheets whipping in the wind across the state and into the rest of our country. The economy could plummet. And, think about the unfathomable cost for clean-up! That is just for California!

Next is the *Indian Point Energy Center* near a fault line 35 miles north of Manhattan, New York. Yes, I said New York. Can you imagine an earthquake *and* a power plant compromised *and then* hit with a tsunami? And, don't think it can't happen. It can. Now, add to this mix that most of our nuclear power plants are old and aging. Like the boiling water reactors at the *Browns Ferry Plant*, located near Athens, Alabama. These reactors are similar to the reactors in Japan and were designed to withstand a 6.0-magnitude earthquake (based on its proximity to the New Madrid fault.) 6.0. Japan's earthquake was 9.0.

Arkansas has a power plant located 150 miles from the San Andréa's fault. As a reference, 150 miles is the radius point Japan was evacuating residents as a result of radiation fall-out.

Of the 55 nuclear plants; including 104 nuclear reactors, in the United States, at least 23 of these plants use a similar reactor to Japan's reactors. To monitor these faults the Federal government created, the *US Geological Survey (USGS)*, but each state has its own state government sponsored geological organization too, to work in tandem with the *USGS* to keep track of geological alterations occurring in each region.

What You Can Do To Prepare

Although the United States has been very lucky (if lucky is even the correct word to use) ... so far, seismologists warn we are overdue for a devastating earthquake somewhere – sometime, in the not so distant future.

If you haven't already done so, you may want to look at a fault-line map of your region to see how prone your area is for earthquakes *and* just how close you live to any nuclear/power plants, while you're at it. Find out your state's geological organization and make a habit of checking for updates on any seismic activity.

When doing your research, take into account wind and water around you as well. Wind can carry radioactive fallout for hundreds of miles. The particles can drop to the ground and into water masses within minutes causing contamination.

Your plan should include, power, fuel, food, and drinking water. Ask yourself. What if you couldn't get out? What if there was water contamination? Would you and your family be okay? If not, you need to begin preparing now. The aftermath of destruction and devastation could make it impossible for you to leave your home or for any help getting to you. Think about your basic needs; food, water, shelter, protection and warmth.

If you do find yourself and family in a situation where there could be radioactive/nuclear fallout; residual nuclear radiation from the plant reactor(s), you need to take the following precautions: limit your exposure to the radiation; properly shield your home or dwelling by taping up windows, vents and doors (if your home has a basement this could be your best option – if not create a containment area in a room, most center, of your house, away from doors, windows and vents, by making a tent-like structure in the room); and, wait for the radioactive materials to decay (up to two-weeks.)

Being isolated for upwards of two-weeks can seem like an eternity. A suggestion would be to include books, puzzles, and game cards to occupy everyone as part of your emergency supplies; thereby avoiding the need to use your socks to make sock puppets! - Just sayin'.

What's Above You Can Hurt You!
CME – What Is That?!

You may have heard or seen the phrase *coronal mass ejection* in the past, and if you are like I once was, you don't have a clue what the heck it means, or what it even refers to. So I am going to put it in simpler terms. I am going to give you a visual explanation of what a *coronal mass ejection* (CME) is that you can probably relate to.

Here goes. Did you ever get a glob of something gooey stuck on your finger; like say a chewed-up sticky piece of gum and you had to shake your hand really hard to fling the gum off your finger? What happened? As you flung your hand the glob on the end of your finger went sailing through the air, right? Well, that is kinda how a *coronal mass ejection* works. During a solar storm on the sun, solar gases and materials in sun spots; which are dark cool areas on the sun's surface, whip out around the sun spot like a bunch of flickering snake tongues – all thrashing about. When one of these *tongues* breaks away it has so much energy that it goes hurling into space in whatever direction the sun spot is facing on the sun. The *hurling energy* part is a *coronal mass ejection* (like the sailing piece of gum). These ejections are huge. I'm talking so big that some of them make our planet look like the head of a pin; *that* kinda huge.

NASA scientists have warned us for some time that if a *coronal mass ejection* were to hit the earth, if large enough, could knock out electricity to the planet – literally. Without getting too technical this is what would happen, as the *coronal mass ejection* approaches earth; usually taking anywhere from one to five days, the resulting force of energy could cause a geomagnetic storm that could knock out electrical transformers and then our power grids – the system that routes our electrical power across our nation.

Think how uncomfortable it is without power during a storm; for a few hours, or even days. Now, think about the nation or even the world being without power! It is really inconceivable isn't it? We would literally be thrown back to the dark ages. The economic damage for our nation alone could be twenty times greater than that of *Hurricane Katrina*. Can you imagine that?

Although to some, this may sound a little science fictiony, in all reality, depending on the 11 year solar cycle (maxima or minima), *coronal mass ejections* can occur once every five days, up to three times a day; so they are not as rare occurrence as you might think. In fact, in 1859 the largest *coronal mass ejection* recorded to date caused a geomagnetic solar storm that took down telegraph systems all over Europe and North America. This event is known as *The Carrington Event*. I know you may be saying "What is the big deal that was a long time ago." So, let's put this event into perspective, if the same type of event happened today – just here in the United States, the damage estimate would be between a half a trillion to $2.6 trillion. That's a lotta dough – which, we don't have.

What You Can Do To Prepare

Preparing for a *coronal mass ejection* (CME) requires having the mindset of your grandparents and great-grandparents. The main reason that people survived The Carrington Event of 1859 was because they were self-sufficient. They farmed, raised and preserved homegrown food and usually

16

got their water from a water-well, stream, or creek. In comparison, our water is pumped in, we purchase our food, and most of our nation's population is all connected to technology - digitally engineered vehicles, home and work appliances and equipment, and all-things-modern-convenience.

If a large *coronal mass ejection*, resulting in a geomagnetic storm, were to hit the U.S., there would be a tremendous amount of damage to our power grid. "So? The power companies will have the power grid back up and running in a few weeks." you say. Well, actually ... no, if transformers are destroyed they would need parts to repair them, parts that are only made in China – yep really. We could literally be thrown back in time for years – or maybe forever.

Just about everything surrounding us today runs on computer technology and electricity. In fact, I'd venture to say everything does; water, fuel, and power.

Ever notice what happens to food in our freezer and fridge when the power goes out? It spoils, right? Think of all the grocery stores and big box stores. They are no different. Their food will spoil without refrigeration too. Gas stations, due to a lack of electricity, will be unable to pump gas, so that means delivery trucks will be unable to make deliveries; that is, even if there was food that wasn't spoiled. And, water? Water pumps wouldn't be able to treat all the sewage – well you get the picture – '*nuf* said. Not to mention, we will all be in total darkness; e-v-e-r-y-w-h-e-r-e with no electricity.

The best thing you can do for yourself to prepare for a coronal mass ejection is to have your basic needs in place. Have water for drinking, and alternative means of water for bathing and washing. Have at least a year's worth of food on hand; canned, freeze-dried, dehydrated and prepackaged (a variety of everything). Keep in mind you will be living your grandparents' life in a broken modern world. There will be no air-conditioning – no central heat – no lights. You will also need to have alternative heat sources, blankets, and a lot of warm clothes to layer with. And, lighting sources such as flashlights, lanterns and, if you must, candles and oil lamps but use these items with abundant caution.

Another thing to consider is that most people will find themselves unprepared, so you will have to protect all your belongings and preparedness supplies, and your family too, from these unprepared people. How you carry this out will be up to you – it's a personal choice, but a must nonetheless. Remember, in total darkness it is possible to see a candle flame from 30 miles away, so even though you thought you were being discreet, you may soon learn you were not. - Just sayin'.

Notes:

The "Bigger" One:
ARk – Storm Bigger Than the "Big-One in California

You may have heard people speak of *the big one* – referencing the San Andreas Fault and a huge earthquake to hit California in the future. But now there is concern about an even *bigger one* for California; a super-storm made of water called an ARk Storm; cleverly named after the boat Noah and his zoo friends sailed in on. The capital *A* and R stand for *atmospheric river* (I didn't want you to think I was getting a little heavy-handed on the cap button!)

To get just a little detailed here; just a little, and for the sake of clarification, *National Oceanic and Atmospheric Administration* (NOAA) has described *atmospheric rivers* as enormous channels, hundreds of miles wide. The storm if it were to happen, would be a near apocalyptic scenario, you know, like the mother of all storms? It would be huge, lasting up to 40 or more days. (Sound familiar?) As the storm sits out in the warm waters of the Pacific Ocean, it can potentially produce rain totals of upwards of 10 feet or even more; which needless to say, would flood huge portions of California. Like I said, if a storm like this were to happen, it would be a catastrophic event, bringing with it devastation on par with *Hurricane Katrina*. Think statewide opposed to citywide, with flooding, landslides, floating debris, erosion, and infrastructure damage.

Much like most natural disasters, an ARk Storm has cycles; usually every other century. And, much like bell bottoms and tie-dyed shirts, the ARk Storm will be making a comeback sometime in the not so distant future.

The driving force behind a storm like the ARk Storm is the charged particles in the atmosphere from the Sun, like with solar flares, CME's, coronal holes, gamma ray burst, and galactic cosmic rays. It sounds kinda Star Warrish, doesn't it? And coronal mass ejections and solar flares are becoming more and more frequent on the Sun. To add to this equation, there have already been biblical-proportion floods recorded in California in 1862 and 1938; and some say in December 2010 as well, so a storm like this can happen.

Now, I'm going to get just a little technical here, the Sun's charged particles that we spoke of earlier, are sometimes called solar winds. These winds produce a flow of particles into the Earth's magnetic field - think dust particles dancing in a Sunbeam of light through a window pane. This flow of particles has a direct effect on the ocean and jet stream currents; our weather patterns. Just thought you'd like to know.

The good news about an ARk Storm - if there is good news when talking about a catastrophic event – is that unlike *the big one* (referring to a San Andreas Fault earthquake), a storm of this size would take days or even weeks to become a reality. Meteorologists will be able to pinpoint the storm's pattern and give us plenty of warning ahead of time. The bad news, well you can imagine, people may not be able to get a flight out once the storm begins because everyone would be vying for those flights out as well. Also, once the storm hits, there would be hundreds of billions of dollars in losses, countless deaths; and the entire state of California could be wiped out.

What You Can Do To Prepare

Your first step in preparing for an ARk Storm is realizing that it is a very real possibility and can happen. Although the flood of 1862 was not an actual ARk Storm, it still caused $10 million in damages – or around $230 million in today's dollars.

There are a lot of flood zones in California, which should tell us something; flooding is as much a part of California as earthquakes are.

Now, as for preparedness suggestions to prepare for an ARk Storm, there have been a lot of infrastructure discussions for bettering flood protection schemes, landslide-hazard mapping, and preparedness for coastal inundation – but as for personal preparedness guidance? Nada, Zip, Zero. All signs point to only awareness.

You might be thinking, "No worry here, I don't live in California so an ARk Storm wouldn't affect me or where I live." Well, maybe yes – or maybe no. Consider this; there are no storm-free zones. The aftermath of an ARk Storm, and its refugees, could spill over into other states across the nation (this is where a natural disaster can turn into a man-made disaster.)

In short, I'm really not sure how a person would prepare for such a storm, lest evacuation to safer, higher grounds?

Or perhaps a boat? Or, water wings? - Just sayin'.

The Sky Is Falling!
The Modern Day Nuclear Attack

Most of us, when we hear the words *nuclear attack* immediately conjure up an image of a huge rocket sailing through the air, hitting a land mass and then bursting into that all too familiar mushrooming cloud. Remember Hiroshima and Nagasaki? People in these areas died of radiation poisoning.

Today a nuclear attack could have far greater implications, especially for us here in the good 'ol U.S. of A. Why? We are far more densely populated now, then in the past, and we are all reliant on the power grid. And, the most eye-opening reason of all, there is a new form of nuclear warfare; an atmospheric nuclear attack.

An atmospheric nuclear attack – is when a nuclear bomb is shot up in to space. The damage and destruction caused by this kind of an attack would be far worse than just a few hundred or possibly thousands of people dying of radiation poisoning. An atmospheric nuclear attack could cripple our country by shutting down our electrical power grid by causing an electromagnetic pulse (EMP).

For those who aren't familiar with what the power grid is, let me explain it this way, say you have a power strip plugged into a wall outlet. Plugged into this power strip is a lighted make-up mirror, a hair dryer, a flat-iron, and a radio. All of these things are heating, playing, and running at the same time. Now think of that power strip as a big power plant and all the items that are all plugged into the power strip as little cities receiving power from the plant. If, the power strip was to come unplugged from the wall outlet, or be switched off, all the power to the lighted-mirror, radio, hair dryer and flat-iron would stop working leaving you with no way to listen to music, or groom yourself (well you could still groom yourself – just not with those items). In other words, you would be helpless without the power the power strip.

The same scenario would hold true, if our nation was struck by an atmospheric nuclear attack or high-altitude nuclear explosion (HANE). The attack would shut our country's power grid down (think power strip), crippling society. A weapon could be shot into earth's atmosphere by a rocket or missile (and much like an atomic bomb that hits a ground target then explodes this weapon is shot into the sky and then detonated causing an electromagnetic pulse (EMP).

The U.S. tested an atmospheric nuclear weapon in 1962. The mission, called Operation Starfish involved a 1.4 megaton warhead attached to a missile and launched 240 miles up into the atmosphere from Johnson Island in the Pacific Ocean; 900 miles from Hawaii. What resulted was a bigger than expect electromagnetic pulse (EMP) that blew out streetlights, and caused widespread telephone outages and radio blackouts in Hawaii. Keep in mind, Hawaii was 900 miles away from the test sight.

What is troublesome about all this is that Russia, North Korea, and Iran are all capable of launching atmospheric nuclear weapons towards the U.S. An atmospheric nuclear weapon could be strapped to a missile and launched over our nation from a shipping container barge sitting out in the Gulf of Mexico.

Think what an EMP attack on our electronically computer driven nation would mean. It would take down our power grid and destroy our electronics networks bringing the world, as we now known it, to a sudden halt. It would be catastrophic.

So how can you prepare for such a strike? Well, there are a lot of little things you can begin doing right away. Let your hair dry naturally (ugh ... I know). Invite your friends and extended family over and practice fixing dinner on your camping stove. Start reading books on how our great grandparents lived and try to mimic what they did. Remember, our great grandparents were living not just surviving – they got along just fine without electricity. You could also get seeds and some plant pots and begin growing some veggies out on your patio or in the backyard.

What You Can Do To Prepare

An atmospheric nuclear weapon attack on our country is a greater possibility today than it has ever been. No longer is the U.S. the powerhouse it once was. Any military arsenal we have, the bad guys now have as well. Our nation has always had a target on its back. All it takes is some crazed maniac launching a missile; which, by the way, could be some surplus rocket with a nuclear weapon attached to it, to take down our nation.

We have all experienced power outages. An atmospheric nuclear attack would cause a nationwide power outage that would last for years – or maybe forever, depending on if and when we could get the parts needed to make repairs.

No matter where you start or how you start, you need to seriously consider that an EMP attack on our country is a

24

very real possibility. Start preparing for the time you may be without electricity.

Ask yourself these things: "Can I go a half a minute without looking at my electronic devices?" "Do I use my debt card for most of my purchases?" "Is my vehicle a later model full of electronic gadgets?" (Note: there are conflicting studies that say due to the electronics in your vehicle an EMP attack may take out your vehicle too leaving it inoperable.)

To see just how reliant you are on electronics, computers and digitally generated items do a simple test. Start in the morning and stop when you go to bed at night. Make a list of *everything* you do. E-v-e-r-y-t-h-i-n-g. This will give you a clear idea of your day-to-day activities. Like me; I wake up and drag myself out of bed (not really I'm one of those jump out of bed people - but I digress.) I turn on the light in the kitchen and make myself a cup of instant coffee (don't judge) using the microwave, water from the faucet and milk from the fridge. I then grab a few eggs; maybe some bacon from the fridge and cook breakfast on the stove top. I then go to the dining room, turn on the light and flip on the TV to watch the morning news as I sit and eat. Once done, I rinse my dishes in the kitchen sink and head to the bathroom, flick on the light, and wash my face in the sink and brush my teeth. As you can see, in this short amount of time, I used a lot of electronics – includes all that running water - all in the span of about 30 minutes. However, I have alternatives for all of these things – just in case.

After an EMP attack, we will not have electronic devices or running water. The value of this test will be to give you a clear idea of your life pattern. Take this list and begin to mimic it by doing most of these tasks by alternative means. Yes it will be difficult at first. But wouldn't you rather be ready by practicing beforehand than be among the desperate after something happens?

You never know when one of those trigger-happy countries may launch an attack. By preparing now, you will also be prepared for later. - Just sayin'.

Notes:

How to Prepare for a Destructive Vortex Of Violently Rotating Winds: Tornado Preparedness

With the increased tornado activity in recent years; and me being a girl from hurricane country, I wondered how the heck a person prepares for a tornado – a vertical hurricane.

I mean, one minute you are sitting on the couch watching TV or doing something around the house and the next minute … *wham* you are dazed, and wandering the debris scattered streets of your neighborhood, wondering where the heck your house went. How does someone prepare for that? What are the *in case of a tornado* rules, guidelines, and procedures?

First, in my research, I learned that no place is exempt from tornadoes. Just because you haven't experienced a tornado before doesn't mean it won't or can't happen where you live. Tornadoes have hit in all 50 U.S. states.

Next, and I know this may sound a bit silly, but if you live in an area where you have never experienced a tornado, you still may want to consider having tornado coverage on your home for a natural disaster such as this (oh yeah, and the zombie apocalypse too - if they will cover you for it.) Some people think that because they have homeowner's insurance, it covers everything. Oh contraire! Many have learned the hard way after a disaster; that this is simply not true. Homeowner's insurance is like purchasing something off of the value or dollar menu at a fast-food restaurant; everything is individually priced. For instance, a hurricane with driving rain hits in your area. There was no structural damage to your home by the hurricane, but the rain puddled and water seeped into your home, damaging the walls and furniture. Not a problem, you think to yourself, I have hurricane coverage. Or so you thought ... not a problem. This damage would be considered flood damage; therefore you would have needed flood insurance to cover the water damage. Having the proper insurance coverage will at least give you some peace of mind that you will have a home to come back to after repairs.

Next, get a National Oceanic and Atmospheric Administration (NOAA) weather-radio and program the radio to all of the surrounding counties around the county you live in - not just the county you live in. The reason you do this, is if you program the radio for only your county, you are hearing about weather that is already there. You know what is headed your way, and have time to prepare and/or make provisions by listening to what is happening in the counties around you. I know it sounds like a pain to listen to what is happening in neighboring counties miles and miles away, but it's always better to know what is going on around you.

So, you have your insurance and weather-radio, now look around the house – both inside and out. A lot of the damage caused during a tornado is by violent winds and flying debris (sometimes in excess of 70 mph or more.) If a tornado can pick up a house and send it down the road, it can easily pickup that bicycle or wagon left out on the lawn and hurl it into a window, which now, leads to the topic of safe places in your home to hunker down in.

Understand, there might not be a completely safe place for you during a tornado, but there are areas that could be safer than others; such as a basement, an inside room without windows, a center hallway, bathroom, or closet. Of course, the place of choice would be a storm cellar – but how many people even have these anymore? If time is not on your side to get to any of these safe areas, get under a sturdy piece of furniture, cover your head and neck with your arms and kiss your … eh, cover your head and neck. Whatever you do, stay away from windows and glass items. That heavy antique vase you inherited from Aunt Gertrude sitting on the mantel may not stay on the mantel, or even in your house. Remember violent winds? And, for goodness sake's don't open your windows thinking you are going to let the winds blow through. It doesn't work that way.

If you happen to live in a mobile home, and a tornado is approaching – needless to say, you need to get to a safe place fast. Don't dilly-dally around. Have an emergency bag packed and ready to go – this goes for all disasters. Growing up in Florida, people referred to mobile homes as *tin cans*. Literally, these homes can have the siding peeled back like someone peeling an orange during a hurricane. And, when gale force storm winds hit them – the home can vanish into thin air leaving a debris field of jumbled, sharp jagged metal, and scattered pieces-parts as far as the eye can see.

How about warnings other than the weather radio? Some tornado prone areas have tornado sirens, but these are outdoor warning systems meant to warn those people who are not undercover to take cover quickly. Also, there is the *sound* of a tornado approaching. People have described it as a loud roar, similar to a freight train. I wonder, how people describe a tornado before the invention of the freight train. Hmm. But I digress. Okay back on task.

Just like hurricane season, there's a tornado season (or seasons). In the southern states the tornado season is March through May, and in the northern states it is during the summer months. But, like all natural disasters, tornadoes have been known to strike any time – anywhere. Always have your emergency bag packed and ready. Keep the bag close by as it might be the only thing – besides you – remaining when the tornado passes.

What You Can Do To Prepare

According to *National Oceanic and Atmospheric Administration* (NOAA) a tornado is one of nature's most terrifying and destructive weather phenomena. It can destroy large buildings, lift 20-ton railroad cars from their tracks, and drive a blade of straw through a telephone pole. Yes, a flimsy blade of straw.

Further, in a typical year, more than 1,200 tornadoes occur throughout the United States. Yes I said, one thousand, two hundred. Unfortunately, we usually only hear about ones that have ripped a town to shreds. But even small tornadoes are destructive to person and property.

Natural disasters can and do happen everywhere. Our weather patterns are becoming more and more unpredictable. Don't let a natural disaster turn into a man-made disaster by you not being prepared.

Tornadoes need pre-planning on your part, as do so many other natural disasters. Start making your plans now. You should have an emergency bag packed for your home, vehicle and at work, with all the personal necessities you would need to help you get by after a disaster. In the bag you should include such things as a shovel, a flashlight, blanket, shoes, underwear, food items, drinking water bottle, and some cash at a minimum.

Oh, and get tornado insurance. It only takes that one rare tornado to leave you homeless.

Have your safe place(s) determined according to where you might be at any given time; home, work, shopping, et cetera. Know what is safe and what is not to hide under, and be sure to steer clear of heavy object that could topple on top of you.

Have a plan for the aftermath of the tornado and where you can stay should your home be destroyed – don't be forced to go to a shelter with hundreds of people because of poor planning on your part. If you do have to leave your home and don't have a safe destination pre-planned nor an emergency bag packed, quickly grab a change of underwear – or two, some emergency cash, a book and stash them into a bag before leaving – you might be at the shelter for the long haul.

Oh, and don't think because you are in an automobile you will be safe. Get out of the automobile; don't try to outrun a tornado in your car. You will lose. Remember the movie *Twister?* the flying cow? the oil tanker? Tornados are violent, vicious winds that leave nothing unturned. - Just sayin'.

❧ 2 ❧
Mental
Preparedness

Following Your Gut Instinct

Walking from the top floor of my high-rise office to the semi lit multi-level parking garage, handbag and keys in hand; my eyes dart back and forth as I watch for the unknown; the hurried driver trying to beat the crowd, a delinquent punk waiting to grab my handbag … or me, or the homeless person who has taken up residence in the garage and is now asking for money. As I reach my car, I notice that someone has placed an advertisement-type postcard on the driver side window. A little perturbed, I snatch the card up and mumble something to myself about hating people being around my car — not because it was a great car mind you, it was just that I didn't like the idea of someone being round my car that's all.

As I unlocked the car door with my key instead of using the car fob, for fear of the battery in it dying leaving me to desperately try and disable the blaring horn as onlookers gawked, a *weird* feeling suddenly came over me. You know that tingly - hair on the back of your neck standing up thing? I quickly got in the car, threw the postcard on the front passenger seat, and immediately locked the doors. Once safe inside, I scanned the floor boards and looked in the back seat … all clear. *Whew!* But that weird *feeling* remained.

Starting my car, I eased out into garage traffic and began my decent; circling round and round from the 6th floor level to the main level while talking on my smartphone to calm my nerves. Finally I reach my destination, the automatic card swiping machine on the lower level. "Ah, home free." I said to myself. But I couldn't shake that darn *feeling*. I swipe my garage card in the machine; the arm raises, and I pull forward to wait my turn for the parting of the sea in traffic so I can pull out on to the road.

Just as I make it to the number one spot, my eye catches two people off to my right running full force down the sidewalk in my direction. My first thoughts were, "These people are probably running to catch a bus or they are in an awful hurry to get someplace." I had two choices and I needed to make one of them fast. I could either pull out across the sidewalk to wait for an opening in the traffic; possibly causing the two men to miss their bus or their important appointment, or I could wait and let them cross in front of me, and then exit out. As is my nature, I chose the latter; I would wait for them to pass in front of my car. It would be my random act of kindness for the day, or so I thought.

What happened next is kinda a blur. The two men I thought I was *helping* had actually just robbed someone at gunpoint at an ATM and were looking for a vehicle to carjack to get away. As the men reached my car, they began to yank hard on the door handles, one at the front passenger door; the other at the back. All I could focus on were those big black guns banging on the windows and that brightly colored yellow bag one of the men was holding in his hand, as they shouted obscenities, and demanded that I unlock the doors.

The irony of it all, is that it was now close to five o'clock rush hour, the roads were already heavy with traffic, and people were beginning to crowd the sidewalks from all directions – oh yeah, and the fact that I was *still chatting* with a family member on my smartphone! I just could not believe that no one was witnessing what was happening or coming to help me. Even the voice on the other end of my smartphone continued to describe their day … in detail, totally oblivious to my frantic cries that *someone was trying to get into my car!* There were people everywhere! Someone had to be seeing what was going on?! It would only be a matter of time before my car windows were smashed in by the gunmen and they would be in the car. All I could think to do was to blare down on my car horn with my hand and not let up in hopes that I could attract some attention my way. Pulling out onto the roadway was not a possibility as I could only turn right or left and traffic was at a standstill pinning me in.

Thankfully, at what seemed like an eternity, but was actually just minutes, I hear the distance and familiar downtown sounds of sirens. In no time law enforcement surrounded my car with their vehicles. The two men hearing the same sounds as me, ran around the back of my car, and were once again running on foot – this time from gun-drawn policemen.

Once the police apprehended and cuffed the men, and took them away, I was free to head home. Shaken, as I drove home, I began to think back on the events that transpired. What was that *weird feeling* I got when I pulled the postcard from the window of my car door that caused me to quickly get in the car, look around, and immediately lock the doors? Normally, I didn't even lock my doors until after I exited the garage and was on the highway. Invariably, I would be *that* person; you know the type, the one whose vehicle is too far away from the card swiping machine so they have to open their car door to reach the machine and swipe their card? My doors didn't unlock automatically when opening them so instead of messing with the locks and trying to open the door, I would just wait to lock them until after I swiped my card and exited onto the road. But on this day that *feeling* said I needed to lock my doors when I got in the car. And, thankfully, I did.

What You Can Do To Prepare

The *weird feeling* I was experiencing, is what is known as a gut-instinct, or intuition. My brain was telling my body that something was not right, and to heed the warning. Gut-instincts, gut-feelings, or intuitions are sudden strong judgments triggered by a belief of something outside. Huh? I know, right? How about this? Intuition is the ability to acquire knowledge without inference or the use of reason. Still not understanding? Okay maybe simpler is better. A gut-feeling or intuition is a response to your subconscious mind after receiving signals from external factors that your conscious mind has yet to pick up on. It means your subconscious mind has picked up on something your conscious mind doesn't see.

I found a postcard lodged in my car door window which triggered my subconscious to respond with a gut-feeling that there could be danger around, although I could not physically see any imminent danger.

These *feelings* can be a hesitation, an odd urge, a hair standing up on the back of your neck -tingle, sweaty palms, a funny feeling in your stomach or even that little voice in your head screaming *stranger-danger* towards a person, event, decision or surroundings.

To explain how this intuition or gut-instinct works, we first need to realize that just because we don't physically see something with our eyes does not mean our brain isn't seeing it. Our *intuitive* right brain is always on the lookout; like a beacon scanning our surroundings, while the conscious left brain is out in *la-la land* oblivious to what is going on around us. The right brain sends messages to our body warning of danger ahead while the conscious mind remains unaware of what's going on.

So how do we learn to recognize these *feeling*? For starters, we can begin by paying more attention to people. Watch for facial expressions or emotional signals (remember how mom always knew when we were fibbing? She watched the expression on our face.)

In a survival situation, it's imperative that we know who we can trust, and who not. The two men I saw running down the sidewalk, in my conscious mind's eye, looked like two people in a hurry, period. But, if I had taken the time to actually look at their faces, instead of talking on my smartphone and watching traffic, I might have seen the urgency in their faces as they looked around for a get-away vehicle. I might have sensed they were bad guys and that I could be in danger.

Watching facial expressions or emotional signals would also be useful in survival bartering with others for something in a poo-hit-the-fan scenario, or after happening upon another group of people. Are they bad guys – do they want to hurt you or take what you have, or are they just like you and your group - trying to survive?

Also, become more aware of these *feelings*. Our subconscious mind has filed all sorts of information away that we don't even recall on a conscious level. It picks up on things like people or events that will trigger that gut-feeling you can't explain. Had I ignored my gut-feeling and not locked the car doors until out on the highway, who knows what, could have happened to me with those two armed and desperate men?

Learn to recognize your *spidey-sense* - that sixth-sense - that tells you something is wrong or dangerous about a person or event, or people acting suspicious, or your safety is in danger.

In a survival and/or disaster situation, especially when the poo-hits-the-fan, your gut-feeling or intuition might be one of your best defenses for protection.

Just as I have, you might one day encounter desperate people who will do desperate things in desperate times. - Just sayin'.

Notes:

I Can't Stress It Enough:
Surviving Under Stressful Conditions

It's a given, we all have *had* stress in our life; some of us more than others unfortunately, at one time or another. And, we all have *felt* stress at one time or another. What exactly is stress and why do we have it?

Stress is our body's way of responding to a demand on it or a reaction to the pressure of certain events or experiences. In other words, it is what we experience when we feel overwhelmed, resulting in a chemical reaction in our bodies - emotions, making it difficult at times to cope.

There is good stress and bad. Good stress, for the most part, can actually help us by inspiring us to meet our daily challenges and, motivate us to reach goals we've set for ourselves. It can also help us do tasks more efficiently and boost our memory. Do you recall that *icky anticipation feeling* before taking a test or giving that speech in front of the class? Remember the hundreds of thoughts running through your head all at once? This is actually the good kind of stress. Our brain is working, using all those resources stored away to help us succeed in whatever we are about to do.

Bad stress, however, can weaken our immune system, and cause high blood pressure, fatigue, depression, anxiety and even heart disease; that is, if we let it go on too long. Think, unpaid bills, house payments, car repairs, job deadlines; relationship conflicts … all of these can cause the type of stress that can physically harm us.

Stress also plays a huge roll in how we deal with a disaster or catastrophic event; before, during and after.

Unfortunately, we can't escape stress – it is a part of who we are, but we can learn how to harness it. Stress is the body's way of rising to a challenge and preparing us to meet a difficult situation; helping us to focus, and giving us strength, stamina, and a heightened alertness. It is hard to grasp, but this kind of stress; stress in a stressful situation, can actually be a good thing. It gives us an understanding of just how much pressure we can handle.

Remember, the test or giving a speech example mentioned above? That *feeling* you get? This kind of stress gives us that extra energy needed to do our best (even though it doesn't feel like it at the time).

On the flip side, stress can also be destructive, and if allowed too, can take over and turn to panic. And, when the panic sets in, all bets are off, and all that preparedness training goes out the window. Not, a good thing.

Have you ever experienced seeing someone who just seemed to crumble in a crisis? Their actions were caused by their fight or flight response. The body prepares itself to fight or flee by producing a shot of energy for whatever decision we make; for some that means doing nothing – thus the crumble part.

We can't let the stressful situations in life get the best of us. (I know, easier said than done.) Remember, our bodies are magnificent machines and are hard-wired to kick into *protection-mode* during stressful times. We need to learn how to harness this stress and use it for our protection and ultimate survival.

What You Can Do To Prepare

During a disaster, I can guarantee you that we are going to encounter a lot of stressful situations – sights, sounds, smells – and stressed-out people. All of these can add to the calamity already going on around us. There will be injuries, sickness, and yes, even death. Now, add to these the matters of inclement weather conditions, scarcity of food, inadequate shelter, unpotable drinking water, and personal safety issues. *Wow!* Just reading this can stress us out! See how quickly our emotions can take over?

Everything you are, and everything you have learned in preparing for survival in a disaster scenario determines what you will find stressful and how you handle that stress. There is no way to avoid stress; especially in a disaster or catastrophic event, but we can tap into this stress and learn to work with it. – Just sayin'.

Notes:

When Things Aren't As Bad As They Said It Would Be

You hear the warnings, a blizzard is coming, a hurricane approaching, floods are imminent, so you go get your vehicles fueled up, buy bottled water, get some cash out of the bank, make a run to the hardware store to get supplies to batten down the hatches, and stop at the grocery store for a few more items for your food supplies. Once set, you hunker down to wait for nature's wrath to rain down upon you. The next day you look out only to realize it wasn't nearly as bad as they predicted.

Soooooo, as human nature dictates, the next time that nature comes calling (no, not *that* type of nature calling), we aren't as gung-ho about preparing as we were in the past, saying to ourselves, "Nothing happened the last time and it was forecast to be far worse than this one." Sound familiar?

Soon we fall into what I call *disaster prepping complacency*. It isn't that you don't believe a disaster could happen or even that it will happen; you just aren't as concerned about it due to your past experiences.

Let's use a shoe analogy, just because a pair of shoes causes a blister doesn't mean you give up wearing shoes altogether, right? You break the shoes in, little by little, by continually wearing them. Same goes with preparedness. Just because something horrible didn't happen when the last *disaster* struck, doesn't mean you stop preparing. Preparedness is an ongoing and evolving process.

Remember the saying "repetition reinforces"? Doing something over and over becomes a habit. Habits become second nature. Am I right?

Think back on the horrible storms of *Hurricane Katrina,* or *Super Storm Sandy,* and the devastating earthquakes in Haiti and Japan. Just about everyone has seen how hurricanes, tornadoes, earthquakes, and other natural disasters worldwide can destroy. But nothing like these disasters or a hurricane like Katrina for that matter, had ever happened in Louisiana. And, nothing like the 9.0 earthquake had ever happened in Japan, either.

Our world is restless. We have far more people now on this planet then have ever been; almost shoulder to shoulder, all trying to get by in life. Some people have the resources to safeguard them against a lot of the fast-balls nature throws our way, but some don't. Those who do, for some, have these resources because of a past experience with a natural disaster and don't want to be caught off guard again. And for the others they know what could happen so they prepare. What when they get ready for an upcoming disaster and nothing happens; as in, they didn't lose power, have any property damage, or weren't locked in, et cetera – everyone begins to go about prepping in a more cavalier approach, thinking, "The last storm wasn't as bad as they said it would be. And this one isn't nearly as bad." Let me tell you, there is a danger in being an armchair storm forecaster – you could become your own worst enemy. Every disaster needs urgency and preparation. This includes both natural and man-made disasters.

What some people don't realize is that many natural disasters can turn into man-made disasters by those who were not prepared for the emergency in the first place. Homes destroyed, walking wounded dazed, no drinking water, gas pipes and water mains broken, power lines down. People become desperate and begin to take ... from anyone, anywhere, any place, and any time.

So just because the natural disaster didn't cause any physical harm to you does not mean you will come out unscathed after the man-made disaster.

What You Can Do To Prepare

I learned the hard way, before jumping on the preparedness bandwagon that after a horrific storm, there is usually no power. That means the gas pumps don't work. Neither do the ATMs, nor the cash registers at grocery stores and restaurants. I was literally shocked by this news, *really*. I mean, it is one thing to have toppled over oak trees, branches and limbs, and trash scattered all around the neighborhood, but to not be able to go buy gas or get money out of the bank, or buy something with your debit card – well that was pretty scary to me. And, a real wake-up call.

Most don't think about these things. I know I didn't, until I was on the shoulder of the road, inching along with the other *clueless* people, waiting to get gas in a ½ mile back up – cash only purchases - mind you. When we hear storm approaching, we focus more on flashlights or candles for power outages, bottled water for drinking, and for the most part, survival food consisting of comfort foods like chips and candy. But gas pumps? ATM? Registers not working? Unfortunately, these usually don't enter the picture. And, as a result, this creates a man-made disaster. People panic when denied their creature-comforts, and easy access to what is normal for them. Entitlement creeps in and they start taking – some with a mindset of "If the cash registers don't work – well then the food and merchandise must be free for the taking." It happens. Or they smell food being cooked on your alternative cooking method … a BBQ grill, wafting through the neighborhood and make a mental note to strike your house when everyone in the household is asleep to take your food. Remember, no matter how nice a person may seem, when they are desperate, they will do desperate things to feed their family, and themselves.

You might also encounter the opportunist. The ones that will take, destroy, or vandalize simply because the opportunity presents itself. No power, under the cover of darkness equates to "no one is looking" or "no one can see me."

As you think about these things, think about putting some money in your emergency bag, and always make sure your gas tank is full; or at a minimum above half … not below, along with water and *real* survival food (which means food with protein) so that you can stay hunkered down and won't have to go out in unsafe areas. Think about foods that don't require a lot of cooking. A huge mistake people make after a disaster is to start cooking everything in their freezer on their BBQ grills to avoid spoilage. This as I mentioned, can backfire and invite unwanted guests to your home by you sending out a *smell-invitation* that you have food.

And, yes, you can pack some candy too; just don't confuse *comfort food* for survival food. - Just sayin'.

Notes:

Band-Aids and Beans and Bullets –
"Oh My"

I remember the first time reading the words, "Band-Aids, beans and bullets" all together in one sentence. I wasn't into preparedness at the time, and was reading a magazine when I came across an article titled "Having your Band-Aids, Beans, and Bullets in order." "Hmm." I said to myself. No worries here, not only are the band-aids in the medicine cabinet in order; arranged large to small, but the cotton balls and gauze are sitting next to the adhesive tape, and the triple antibiotic ointment is at the ready with the bottles of peroxide and alcohol close by. In fact, the medicine cabinet is neat, orderly, and readily accessible for all those to frequent *kitchen disasters* of mine, like cooking burns or slicing accidents. And, as for my pantry, the beans are in order and well organized according to what kind of beans they are. So, yes, my band-aids and beans are in order!

Now, the bullet thing ...? Well, that was a toughie for me. I didn't have a clue about "ah" bullet, let alone a bunch of bullets, or how to put them in any kind of order. So, I just chalked it up to it being a guy thing.

Had I read the article, I would have learned that having your *band-aids, beans, and bullets in order* is a preparedness euphemism that means having your emergency supplies in order. Band-Aids represent first-aid and having all the medical supplies and equipment needed for any foreseeable injury or illness during and after a disaster or catastrophic event; which yes, includes band-aids. Band-Aids is the catch-all for any and all medical supplies; along with the

46

knowledge of how to use these medical supplies, in your emergency medical kit.

Beans represent our food supply (including water.) This would encompass any and all types of foods; freeze-dried, dehydrated, or dried, tin can, preserved, prepackaged, spices, herbs, seasonings, condiments, all-things-preparedness food. It also includes different cooking methods to cook your food, all the utensils, and cookware needed to do so, and water, and all the different ways to contain, clean and filter the water. In other words, anything and everything we could possibly need to provide sustenance in a disaster or catastrophic event.

And bullets, how do they relate to preparedness? Bullets represent any and all means to protect and defend yourself, your family, your property, your food and medical supplies.

We have all probably weathered a storm or two, albeit snow, ice, hail or even a hurricane. And with these events, we may have also dealt in the inconveniences of having no power for a few days or more. Think back to those times. Remember how you scurried around trying to find candles and matches, or flashlights when the power went out? Do you recall stubbing your toe in the darkness because you couldn't see where you were going? If your emergency supplies had been in order, you would have known exactly where the candles, matches, and flashlights were stored and would not have used precious battery time hunting for the band-aids and antiseptic ointment to treat your injured toe afterwards.

Having band-aids, beans and bullets in order, means not having to scurry around trying to find your emergency supplies during a disaster or emergency. It also means having all your basics needs ready for those unknown times; food, water, medical supplies, and a means of protecting yourself and your property.

Survival basic needs are the cornerstones of your preparedness plan foundation. We all know what happens when we build something on a weak foundation, don't we? The foundation will crumble under pressure.

What You Can Do To Prepare

Preparedness planning can be confusing at times. What are you preparing for? How much of any one thing should you have? There are so many questions that need answers. This is why preparedness experts try to make it easier for those who are just starting out by creating acronyms and little phrases or sayings. But, what happens, as in my case when I began my journey into preparedness, I spend more time trying to decipher these little sayings than actually doing any preparing. Sometimes, we just need to look beyond the literal to understand the practical of what is being said. I'm sure it was someone's hope that by using the cleaver *B* words in a phrase that it would help people remember the *basic* needs of survival better. (Look more B-words!) And, for some I'm sure it does help. For me, unfortunately, I took this article to mean be neat and tidy, and so could other people who are just starting out in preparedness.

The intent of these phrases is to remind us to focus on the meaning or the message behind the phrase or phrases; which is, the importance of having all your basic needs of survival in order, with food, water, shelter, protection, warmth, fire, first-aid and communication, before a disaster, so that desperation won't set in and you find yourself scurrying around at the last-minute with all the other unprepared trying to vie for whatever is remaining on the store shelves.

Remember this, it is more common to die due to a lack of preparation, then it is from the disaster itself. – Just sayin'.

Notes:

What If Tomorrow a Disaster Really Did Happen? Preparing Today for Tomorrow

I read one day, about someone dying while at work. Not by some horrific industrial-type accident, but from something that had apparently gone undetected in his body for years. This man woke-up on the morning of his death, showered, got dressed, ate breakfast, grabbed a to-go cup of coffee, his newspaper, and headed to work … to die. It was just one of those fluke things that happen in life - to some - an unknown that just appears out of nowhere and snatches life from you.

This news really struck me hard. How sad to be at work, doing something you really enjoy doing, and you just die. I began to wonder who in a million years would have thought this could have happened. Not me – and I'm sure not this man – if anyone at all. I wondered if someone had shared with this man; the man who died at work, (you know, like you could open the window to the future) that he was going to die this way, would he have done something - could he have done anything, differently? Could he have been more prepared to prevent his death? Sadly, that is just not how life is sometimes.

Continuing to think more about the future, I realized, the window of the future is actually opened for those people who are preparedness-minded. We *know* that our life could end by a predictable or unpredictable disaster or catastrophic event and so we have taken steps in an attempt to save ourselves.

So what about all the other people out there? Why aren't they doing more? Are they clueless? lazy? complacent? Are they waiting for someone else to do it for them? Are they thinking someone is going to come and save them?

Unfortunately, if a disaster happens, most people will be more concerned about themselves than they are about saving other people. Therefore, we have to prepare for ourselves, by ourselves.

Looking back to the Y2K scare, and I say scare because at the time it scared the bejeezus outta me, I learned; after-the-fact mind you, that a lot of people prepared for *the next day* or *the end of the world as they knew it* by having emergency supplies and survival water and food. I remember that time, but not like they do. I wasn't prepared I was scared. I heard bits and pieces of conversation, here and there that all the computers were going to crash or fail at midnight on New Year's Eve, resulting in a total collapse of society and the economy around the world. I really didn't understand the full extent of what they were saying, and frankly, I didn't know what the heck a *total collapse of society* even meant. There was no measure to comprehend the magnitude of the prediction. I knew nothing about computers, and even less about world events, the economy, or politics. All I could grasp from what I heard was that something very bad was going to happen on New Year's Day 2000.

On New Year's Eve, with a nervous stomach, I stayed up to watch the ball drop, not for entertainment, but for my safety. I was afraid to go to sleep. I was waiting for the ball to drop (the bewitching hour), and I guess the next shoe to drop as well. What would the next day bring? I watched and listened as the jovial hosts; above the loud chatter of thousands of people on the streets below, announced as each country brought in their New Year. I remember wondering at the time why all those people were there and not at home with their loved ones. Thankfully, nothing really happened throughout the night and a good thing too, because if life as we knew it had ceased on New Year's Day, I could have been one of the hundreds, perhaps thousands or even millions of refugees walking the streets, hunting for food and water.

What You Can Do To Prepare

Looking back, what concerns me most about the Y2K scare, is just how many people; including myself, were absolutely clueless about what *could have happened*, and for many, this is still true today. We could still be facing a possible collapse of society or the economy; unpredictable inclement weather trends and unemployment; among other things, and yet most of us still go about our day oblivious to what could actually happen – in our very near future.

Is it because, like we had for Y2K, we don't have a specific date for a disaster? And, if not, what could it be? Why aren't we doing more to save ourselves?

With or without looking through the *window of the future* we know that flooding, earthquakes, tornadoes, hurricanes and snow/ice storms have been the worst we've seen in decades – as are the economy, housing market and unemployment.

If you could save yourself and that of your loved ones, would you? Of course you would! But you're not. – Just sayin'.

Notes:

Words Can't Describe It:
Visualizing a Disaster

Has anyone ever described something to you, but when you actually saw it for yourself it was, eh, bigger, smaller, worse, better, (fill in the blank) than what was actually described to you? The reason this may happen, is because when we hear something described, our mind conjures up a picture, an image, from our memory banks of what we think the person is describing. For example, if we have never seen a big lion up-close, like at a zoo or an attraction, and we hear someone who describes their experience with a lion; our mind can only guess what the lion looked like, or how big it was, or even how it smelled. Am I right?

The same could hold true when we read survival and preparedness books and articles as well. Without having a point of visual reference, the same thing happens. We are merely guessing as to what is being said or described.

One of the many ways I work at being more visually prepared, is I watch movies on apocalyptic and post-apocalyptic events (before and after a disaster or catastrophe). Sure the movies have great computer-generated graphics to really *Hollywood* them up, but what I try to do is to focus on the disaster itself, and the characters in the movie. How do the characters react to what is going on? What are they actually doing to survive? I watch movies as a point of reference, to see and hear what a disaster could be like.

When watching these apocalyptic movies, it amazes me what people will do in desperation. Good people and bad people, it makes no difference, we are all human beings and are unpredictable in times of stress, which usually leads to violence. People will inflict unspeakable harm on one another for the sake of their own survival and ... that of a can of beans. These are the parts in the movie, I used to close my eyes at, but soon realized that this was counter-productive to the reason I was watching the movies in the first place – not just for the love interest of the characters in the movie, but for what hard times will look like. These movies are scary to the point of realizing that these scenarios could actually happen or be our world in the near future. Sadly, for most of the people watching these movies, it is pure entertainment.

There are a lot of these apocalyptic and post-apocalyptic movies. If watching them is too confusing or scary at first, you might want to pick a movie that you like the actor who stars in the movie for starters – it will make it a lot easier initially to watch them. Once you've conditioned yourself a little more, you can move on to others, and watch them like a true prepper!

What You Can Do To Prepare

There are many factors that play a role in determining what turns into a memory; among them is how much attention we pay to a particular activity, how interesting it is, and what evokes an emotion. Visual memories are the recollection and retrieval of those memories.

By watching dystopian, apocalypse and post-apocalypse movies or reading books on these topics; when focusing on them for survival skills, and how people react in panic situations, we are burning these things into our memory banks. Then, when we find ourselves in danger, we can pull what we have mentally stored, so we can respond or react from our memories.

Personally, I don't foresee some of the issues or conditions that come up in some of these apocalyptic books and movies; they are too far-fetched for me, but until a catastrophic event occurs, we will never know. I mean, right? (So, I'm not discounting anything!)

By seeing, hearing and reading about disasters, and apocalyptic events, we can file these important sights and sounds into our memory banks, to fall back on, as a future reference. It's like a conditioning exercise for your mind.

And, if it's a movie you are watching ... there is a bonus, you get to eat popcorn while you're watching it! (Well you could eat popcorn while reading too but ... you will get butter all over the pages!) – Just sayin'.

Notes:

I Think I Can – I Think I Can:
Mental Preparedness

Mental preparedness is just that, mentally preparing your mind for whatever may come your way as part of your preparedness plan.

Take a moment and think about this question. "Where are you *mentally* regarding the knowledge and skills needed for any kind of disaster?" Granted, you may know what the survival necessities are for a disaster situation; such as supplies, a good place to shelter in and the need for protection, but have you actually played-out a disaster scenario in your mind? In other words, mentally rehearsed a disaster by visualizing yourself in that disaster?

Personally, I have never been shot at, or been grabbed and pulled into an ally, but I have played this scenario out over and over in my mind, hundreds of times.

Your mind begins to accept things as reality and soon it becomes automatic or second nature without a conscious thought, by focusing on a situation or situations, and what you would or could do to protect yourself. Then, should something bad happen in the future, and you find yourself in harm's way, your mind not knowing the difference between reality and memory, kicks into action retrieving the skills needed to help you survive. The concept is called *muscle memory*.

Memories we store in our brain, drawn from repetitive thinking or by doing something over and over. Like when you drive a car. Have you ever been driving someplace and arrived at your destination and didn't remember going past the school, the bank, or the stop sign? This was your muscle memory taking over. Your subconscious knew the driving routine without you consciously thinking about where you were going. It was a repetitive habit (scary too, huh?)

If you think you can, you can, period. Your mind doesn't know the difference. In other words, if you can see it in your mind, you can do it.

Creative visualization works together with positive self-talk and affirmations. Just as you can talk yourself out of something, you can talk yourself into it as well.

What You Can Do To Prepare

Albert Einstein once said, "Imagination is more important than science." Wow, then I must be a genius! I spent more time in science class daydreaming then I did on science. Okay, okay, I'm sure that is not what Einstein meant, but my point being is we need to read, watch, talk and learn as much as possible on disaster preparedness and what to do, or not do, during and after a disaster. Visualize images of everything and everyone along the way.

Watch what other people do and don't do. What they say … and don't say. How they respond or react to a given situation. Condition your mind to think about these things as others did and then as you would in a similar situation.

The name for kind of practice thinking is called *visualization*. It's the practice of recreating all the images, sounds, and feelings in your mind of a particular activity.

Every time you read an article on a disaster, visualize yourself in that scenario as the author is describing it. When you watch a disaster genre television show or movie, become one of the characters, focus on what they say or do – or what they don't do or say in response to something. How did they defend themselves? Take mental notes, or even physically write things down, and then later visualize yourself doing these things.

Think about this for a moment, if you read dystopian, apocalyptic, and post-apocalyptic books purely for the entertainment value, and don't visualize yourself as a part of the story you could be missing out on a huge opportunity to prepare for a life-threatening event, without physically doing anything. Most of us have never experienced the things conjured up in the imaginations of these authors, but when such a disaster does rear its ugly head, we may find that we are now one of the survivor characters in that book we read, or the character who does not bode so well.

Preparedness requires practice. Ask anyone who is the best-of-the-best and they will tell you that they achieved their skills by constantly performing them over and over. And when they were not physically performing their skills, they were mentally visualizing themselves doing them, or watching others, and trying to emulate them.

Physical and psychological reactions to certain situations can improve with visualization. This repeated imagery can also build confidence to do certain skills under pressure too. Always remember this, repetition re-enforces, which means, the more you do something, the better you will be at it. Yes, even if you have never done it before. So start daydreaming! – Just sayin'.

Notes:

Life Is A Stage:
Practicing for Your Survival

Okay, you have been physically trained and re-trained on how to defend yourself, from awareness of your surroundings, to self-defense, to weapon use, and so on and so forth. Then, when you least expected it; as is usually the case when confronted with a threat of harm, instead of kicking butt like you were trained to do … you freeze.

What the heck happened to all that training? Why instead of reacting you froze? Your survival instincts should have kicked in – but they didn't. Why? You mentally froze.

In times of trouble, you could be alone out there on the big stage we call life. It will be up to you, and you alone, to perform like your life depended on it … because it might. You may not do that karate kick exactly the way the far more experienced and seasoned instructor taught you to do it, or hit your target where you intended to, but you must react, you can't just stand there.

We have all heard this *freeze* thing described in a lot of different ways; like for instance, the ol' deer in the head-lights syndrome? It's like someone flips a switch and there you are standing with that dumb-blank stare thing going on. This phenomenon actually has a name for it. It's called hyper-vigilance. And, it is more common, than you may think when placed in a defensive situation. There are several factors going on in our brain that causes us to *freeze-up*. One is, not really knowing what to do in the situation. Another is, not trusting our abilities.

Remember the flight or fight response? It's the physiological reaction that occurs in response to a perceived harmful event, attack, or threat to survival. It is our body's automatic early warning system, pre-wired (no downloading necessary) that prepares us to either fight or ... well run like heck to survive. In a slit second, our brain will analyze the situation, and will pick a solution based on our knowledge, experience and training, and respond back in kind – with a focus on nothing more than short-term survival.

As we perceive danger, our heart beat quickens, we begin breathing faster, and our entire body becomes tense and ready to take action. A shot of adrenaline and other stress hormones rush through our body, and if for only for a short time, we are more powerful than a locomotive and able to leap tall buildings in a single bound – well for some. What also happens is we are able to think creatively, but at the same time, our logical thinking is dramatically impaired.

When danger is imminent, both our short-term and long-term memories play a huge part in how we will react. If a person is well-trained, in say, self-defense, then the brain will most likely draw from the short-term memory. But, if they are facing something they have never experienced before, or defended themselves against, and aren't sure how to react, the long-term memory must scroll through all of their past knowledge and experiences for the right response. This is where the *freezing* part during a time of danger comes from, your brain does not have an answer and must go and find one – and sometimes can't.

What You Can Do To Prepare

So, how can someone remedy a *freezing* response in time of danger? First, we need to understand that the *freezing* response in and of itself, is also a common response to fear, and is another survival mechanism. This freezing could be just as important as the fight or flight response. For instance, let's say we are walking down the street, and just as we are about to round a corner, we see two bad-guys running towards us who have just beaten-up and robbed someone. By us freezing (staying put) instead of jumping out all *kung-fu like*, we can possibly avoid being harmed ourselves. The bad guys (hopefully) will assume we didn't see a thing and run right past us perceiving us as non-threatening (though we know better with all that kung-fu fighting training of ours.) So, when the fight or flight response is not an option – the freeze response kicks in, as our last line of defense.

The best way to practice your responses is to program your brain to memory, to know what to do and how to react in any given situation. Like computers, our brains are just gonna sit there until we either input something, or try to retrieve something.

Just as we would practice our lines, before going out on stage for a live performance, we must practice our *what-if* scenarios too. Play them out in your mind and use different tactics and methods in each scenario so you have options that the brain can retrieve when called upon to do so. Get self-defense training, which teaches you not only how to protect yourself, but also how to evade, or even de-escalate potential dangerous situations.

If you do freeze-up in a not so right time for freezing up, (remember this is an unconscious decision made by your brain when it cannot find a remedy for the situation), take a moment to calm down – a moment, as in a few seconds. This will allow you to get control over your thoughts again so you can respond. Breathing helps clear your clouded mind from the process of trying to figure out what to do next. Now, breathe. – Just sayin'.

Notes:

What's So Golden about a Golden Horde?

Now, now don't get all excited, I'm not talking about golden as in coins or bullions (I know, ah nuts!), I am referring to "The Golden Horde." From what I understand, the term "The Golden Horde" was originally given to Turksicized Mongol Rulers who flourished from the mid-13th century to the end of the 14th century; but that's a history lesson for another day. What I want to talk about is what has become synonymous with post-disaster refugees.

The Golden Horde as it pertains to a disaster scenario refers to a mass exodus migration of people who flee the aftermath of a catastrophic event in search of food, water, and shelter. It could be from an earthquake, a hurricane, an EMP attack, a flood, and even an economic collapse, and later, civil unrest. You name it – anything that totally wipes out the infrastructure of a neighborhood, city, town, state … or *(gulp)* our nation could result in The Golden Horde.

A mass exodus of refugees, after a disaster, would more likely than not, occur initially from inner cities; much like what we saw happen during *Hurricane Katrina*. People who were not prepared for any type of disaster, or displaced by the disaster, would most likely take to the highways and roads, by whatever means available. If by vehicle; the amount of gas in their tanks, and whether gas stations were capable of pumping gas, might determine how far a person got before having to abandon their vehicle and continue on foot. (Not to mention gridlock traffic.)

Now consider this, a city usually has many entrances and exits throughout the city to get you around town; east, west, north and south and, all those directions in between.

At any given time in the normal course of a day there could be hundreds, possibly thousands of vehicles on these roads – eventually though, people will abandon vehicles either due to the gridlock or empty gas tanks. Should the interstates be gridlocked; which I can assure you they will be, the alternative would be to head for the highways and what I call 'back roads' or rural and secondary roads. Can you imagine all those people? Think an ant farm. All those people like ants, tunneling in every direction, weaving in and out – passing one another. That is what a mass exodus would look like from a bird's eye view!

Here's another scary thought. Most cities in recent years have turned into mega cities - that is, the population is in excess of 10 million people. Ten m-i-l-l-i-on!! Imagine 10 million people, okay even one million people, trying to get out of just one city in all directions! (And we think we have it bad in traffic jams after a huge concert or sporting event let's out – and even then we are usually only dealing with a few thousand people!) It is truly mind-boggling to even try to imagine all the people who will be walking, driving, pushing/pulling carts, wagons, strollers, shopping carts, all carrying with them whatever belongings they could gather, all trying to get out of the city and to who knows where?

There are so many variables about how far someone will actually get. Some will get to the nearest town. Some will push on. Some will get no farther than a few blocks from their homes. But one thing is for certain, these people will be hungry, tired, and thirsty – and eventually will become angry – some will be people used to the government taking care of them, some white-collar workers, some blue-collar workers – but the one thing they will all have in common is the need to take care of themselves and their families. This, is when desperation will set-in, and could lead to people doing desperate things, like looting, stealing and yes ... killing someone if need be.

What You Can Do To Prepare

I have always stressed, and will continue to do so, that we need to have our emergency go-bags packed and ready to grab and go. We may find that we too will be one of those on foot not able to jump in our vehicle and head out as planned. So, make a plan for this contingency now. Take the time to pull out a map or your area and begin looking at all the routes in and out of your neighborhood, your city, and yes even your state. Create an exit strategy of routes less traveled; those little unknown ways to get to places that most don't use or even know about. Start searching for them now. It may mean traveling at night and through wooded areas, so you will need adequate clothing, footwear, lighting, and protection. Taking the path that is less traveled may take longer to get to a safe destination, but by planning ahead you will be far better off than the others who did not plan at all and have become a part of The Golden Horde. As you can see, The Golden Horde is not so golden after all. - Just sayin'.

Notes:

What a Great Personality:
Knowing You Disaster Personality

Author, Amanda Ripley's book "The Unthinkable: Who Survives When Disaster Strikes - And Why?" was a huge eye opener for me. In her book the author writes, *"In moments of total disaster something happens in our brains that affects the way we think. We behave differently, often irrationally."* This statement hit me right between the eyes … because it is so true! *Wham!* The writer goes on to say that each of us has what she calls a *disaster personality* - a state of being that takes over in a crisis. It is at the core of who we are.

Think back on an emergency big or small in your past that you've watched unfold before your eyes or you personally experienced. It could be as simple as a pot boiling over on the stove, to someone being seriously injured from a chainsaw accident, to a horrific traffic accident. Now, think about how you reacted or responded to it.

I actually, witnessed a woman refusing to take off her 4" designer heels to walk down 16 flights of stairs during an office fire?! Apparently, her core told her that her shoes were far more important than her life, right?! News Flash: After walking down about two flights of stairs, and people pushing their way around her, mumbling for her to take off her *darn* shoes (or other expletive words), the woman kicked off her shoes and walked down barefooted. Priorities, right?!

In her book, the author searched for patterns in human behavior by interviewing hundreds of people who lived through catastrophic events. What she discovered was all of us undergo a three-stage process when we find ourselves in a life threatening situation: denial, deliberation, and decisive moment.

How many of you have heard the fire alarm go off at your workplace and continued to work anyway? – Denial. Then, you learn someone burnt some food in the microwave on another floor. "It's not on our floor so I'm staying put." you say – Deliberation. Smoke begins to fill in through the air vents into the office, you grab your keys and cell phone and head for the nearest emergency stairs (hopefully kicking off any heels on the way out) – the Decisive Moment.

According to Ms. Ripley, there are five ways to refine our disaster personality, attitude, knowledge, anxiety level, body weight, and training. First, attitude, people who do well in crises tend to have three underlying advantages; they believe they can influence what happens to them, they find meaningful purpose in life's turmoil, and believe they can learn from both a good and bad experiences. Next, knowledge, the brain is amazingly acceptable. If you understand how you are likely to react to a disaster situation, you can learn to override your worst instincts – or train your brain to respond to them in a more positive way. You can train your brain to interpret things differently, which means you will most likely be calmer in the face of a crisis in the future, by learning what your real risks are, or the risks that concern or scare you the most. Then, there is anxiety level. People with higher everyday anxiety levels may have a greater tendency to freeze or totally shut down in an emergency. That is not always a bad thing. In fact, it's a very common reaction. But it's important to recognize this tendency in us and override it.

Next, body weight (I know, I am treading lightly here.) The harsh truth is that overweight people move more slowly and are more vulnerable to secondary injuries; like fatigue, heat exhaustion, or heart attacks. And, lastly, training, by far, the best way to improve yourself and your chances of survival is to practice. It could be running, hiking, climbing up steep inclines, walking long distances, going without food or water for a day, staying out in the heat ... or cold, carrying a heavy backpack around (a good time to practice carrying your emergency bag *hint*), or camping with minimal supplies (that means forgetting about that cooler full of cold drinks) - minimal ... think survival.

So, remember attitude, knowledge, anxiety level, body weight, and training – are all areas to help us strengthen our disaster personality.

What You Can Do To Prepare

First of all, we need to put these five ways to redefine a disaster personality to memory. Again, they are attitude, knowledge, anxiety level, body weight, and training. Please note: that we are not expected to do all of these - no one is. They are simply a way to strengthen us and help us understand where our personal disaster weaknesses are.

Try to figure out what your own personal disaster personality is. And, begin to focus on the specific areas you are weak in. Use past experiences as a guide. Are you the type of person who jumps up on a chair if a big bug comes crawling across the floor, or if you see a spider do you whack the daylights outta it? When you see someone injured and bleeding profusely, instead of rushing to their aid, do you head in the opposite direction? If you had to use a firearm to protect yourself or your family – would you shoot to maim or shoot to kill? Or, worse yet, be so frightened that you end up shooting yourself?

Begin to practice these five areas of improvement, by making a list of the biggest risks around you in the region you live and in the normal course of your everyday activities; think different types of disaster situations, big and small to give your brain a starting reference.

Consider the three stages we go through when faced with an impending disaster. Denial - "Ah, nothing happened. Someone just pulled the alarm." Deliberation - "This is only a drill. I'm going to stay put. I'm not walking down all those flights of stairs." And, the Decisive Moment - "Holy cow there is a fire! I gotta get outta here!" These stages can all play out in a matter of seconds and *everyone* is going through them all at the same time.

I'm sure we all would agree, most of us love being around a person with a great personality. Am I right?? Especially if it's a great disaster personality!! – Just sayin'.

Notes:

Get Your Head Outta the Sand People!
How to Share Awareness about Disasters

I once read a national survey that addressed personal preparedness here in America. The survey was designed to evaluate the nation's progress on personal disaster preparedness, and to measure the public's knowledge, attitudes, and behaviors as it pertained to a multitude of disasters. The responses, to say the least, were shocking and eye-opening to me. To put it bluntly, we are living next door to a bunch of ... well idiots!

As an example, although 78% of those who responded actually believe that disaster preparedness, planning, and emergency supplies would help them in a natural disaster, 4 out of 10 of these people felt it wouldn't make any difference. And, 27% said they were not planning to do anything about preparing!! Not anything at all?! Zip!! Zero! Nada! And their reason was? (Drum roll please.) 40% said they believed emergency responders would come and help them! (i.e., save them) Are you kidding me?? Yeah, look how that turned out with *Hurricane Katrina* and *FEMA*!

Now, how about this one? 37% of those surveyed thought a natural disaster would *never* affect their community. Where the heck do these people live that would exclude them from a disaster? I mean, really? I want to live there too! To be honest, I didn't even know there was such a place that precluded you from any kind of disaster? Did you? Where is this place, do tell? A cave?

If these statistics are surprising to you, this one really got me. Less than one in five believes there is any threat of an act of terrorism in their communities. *"Holy-moley!"* I

72

screamed down at the page ... What part of terrorist don't you understand? *Terrorist: one-who-creates-terror.* And, who now live inside and outside this country? Look at all the *terror* that has happened in our country! No threat? I mean, really?

These responses are absolutely scary. And, they confirm just who the people are that live next to us, work with us, go to church with us, and socialize with us. Are these people so stuck in *reality television world* that they aren't paying attention to events around them? Do they think because they don't pay attention that they are not accountable?

Bad things do happen in this country and are happening more and more every day. Unfortunately, as a nation and even in our communities we are underestimating these potential threats.

First responders; policemen, fire-fighters, EMTs, et cetera, are people just like you and I. They aren't superheroes; they are hardworking people who try to save lives and help people. In a disaster, they will only be able to do what they can. If there is gridlock on the roads, due to panicked drivers, emergency responders will not be able to get to you or your community, due to the impassable roads. This is exactly what happened in Texas with *Hurricane Rita.*

Disasters bring on chaos, panic, and confusion for everyone. Learn to respond not react. It's time for us to encourage more people to pull their heads out of the sand (or wherever their head happens to be lodged), and come up for air.

It seems there are just not enough of us who even consider a disastrous event as a possibility in our future.

What You Can Do To Prepare

If you have friends, neighbors, loved-ones or family members who are not prepared, it is important that you do not enable them as you attempt to help them understand the importance of disaster preparedness. What I mean by this is, don't give them a *free pass* just because they aren't on the *preparedness bandwagon.* Remember these are the same people who may very well end up on your doorstep after a disaster.

A great way for you to ease these non-preparedness minded people into preparing is with entertainment (sheeple-people are more into fun-loving activities - doing fun things.) Give them a good action-packed dystopian book that portrays the characters in a catastrophic event. Or invite them over for movie night – a real nail-biting apocalyptic/post-apocalyptic thriller.

How can books and movies help someone get more prepared? You are subtly planting subliminal preparedness seeds by using post-apocalyptic genres. And, you are opening the doors of opportunity for conversations about disasters. Ask these non-prepared friends and family questions like, "What would you do if you were (name a character in the book or movie.) Play along too and add in your two-cent worth. Get them thinking about how a disaster such as what they just read about or saw in the movie are not so far-fetched after all. Use current disasters from around the world as examples to show that what they read or saw can actually happen; and why it's important to have a *few things put aside* for these disasters.

Don't expect a transformation to happen all at once after watching a movie or reading a book. At first your friends might be more fascinated with the great computerized graphic affects or the gruesomeness of the bad-guys' actions, then about the disaster itself. Don't get frustrated. Have patience. Being oblivious to what is going on is a lifestyle-mentality. It's a habit, a comfort zone. You are asking your friends and loved-ones to step out of their *happy place* and face a not so happy subject. – Just sayin'.

Notes:

❧ 3 ☙
Self-Defense

Hey Gimme That!
When What You Have Is Taken

We scrimp and scrape, to save money, so we can buy items we think we may need for a disaster; personal, natural and man-man, or heaven forbid, a catastrophic event where life as we knew it would be no more. Proudly gazing at our wares, pleased in our minds at least, we can survive any given number of disaster scenarios.

Okay so you have your survival items, but, let me ask a question. Have you given any thought to how you are going to protect all these goods you purchased? I mean, think about it. The world is split between the *haves* and *have-nots*. We are the *haves* - the people who have painstakingly put their needs before their wants to assure some semblance of survival should a disaster or catastrophic event happen. The people who know that our government is not equipped to come and save us should a disaster strike. And who know from history and experience that we may well be headed for some earth shattering events, such as a nuclear terrorist attack, on our homeland in the not so distant future. Then, there are those who say they will deal with whatever happens, when it happens. Those people are the '*have-nots*.

Have-nots go all the way back to infancy. For example, put two toddlers in the same playpen or room full of toys and invariably one will want the toy the other is playing with, even with a bazillion other toys lying around. Why is that? Because each toddler believes everything belongs to them. So then what happens? Well, usually a battle-of-the-wills ensues beginning with the first *mine* echoed by a countered 'no-mine'. Now, flash forward to elementary school and the playground, where in my opinion, most bullies learn to hone their skills; the skills that will continue, sometimes, well past school days into college, work, the night club scene, personal relationships, and yes even into their marriage. Don't get me wrong. I am not saying that all 'have-nots' are, or have been, bullies in the past and taking by intimidation. What I am saying is that there is a good percentage that I can bet were, and still are.

Most 'have-nots' will be a mixture of bad people, desperate people, hungry people, and yes, even good people – all with a desire to survive and therefore, will do whatever it takes to do so. Yes, I said good people too. No one, and I mean no … one, will be exempt from attacking another when their survival or that of their loved ones is at stake.

In a catastrophic event, you will find there will be those who take for different reasons. Some because they don't have, such as the golden horde or zombie refugees, those who take for power; such as the Government, and those who take because they can; such as outlaws, bad guys, or rebels.

So what the heck can we do about protecting ourselves? You might even be thinking "What's the use in preparing or having food, water and survival gear if someone is going to come barging in and take everything anyway from us?" And therein lays the answer. Not only do you need food, water and survival gear, but you need a way to protect these items, and yourself from the *have-nots*.

There are safeguards you may want to start, and merge into your survival strategies and preparedness plans. First, and foremost, don't announce to the public everything you have accumulated. And, by the public I am referring to anyone outside your immediate family. What do I mean by this? Well, don't tell Mary at her baby shower that the dessert you made was from your food storage, and when questioned more, you also tell her you have a whole basement full of food and supplies for if a disaster strikes, which is overheard by Debbie, who invariably tells her husband Mike when she gets home, who then, while hanging with the guys at work one day and gets on the topic of zombies, tells them what his wife told him about a family up the street who has stockpiles of food, ... and so on and so forth. See where I'm going?

In your mind, you only told one person. But, who do you think will be at your doorstep after the desperate have-nots have ransacked all the groceries stores and cleaned them out of food and water? My bet is on the husbands of Mary and Debbie ... and their buddies - that's who. It will go something like this, Debbie's husband comes home from forging and tells his wife that there is nothing left in the stores; and there is no food anywhere. Debbie then says to her husband, "Remember the friend at a baby shower I told you about? She has a lot of food stored in her basement. I know she will give us some, they are such nice people. Why don't you just go over there and ask?" Or, the wife of one of the buddies that Debbie's husband told about the food in the basement, panics. "There's no food left in the house ... what are we gonna do?" she cries to her husband. The husband then tells her, "Mike told me about a lady that lives around here that has hoarded all kinds of food. I'm going to go over there and get us some."

Or, there it could even be a public announcement from the local Government, which says in part, that anyone with food and drinking water is required to turn it all over to the authorities so it can be distributed to everyone equally. Law Enforcement will be going door-to-door to collect the food and water. "Wait they can't do that!" you say in protest. And, the ugly truth of the matter is, by Executive Order, yes they can ... and will.

Any one of these scenarios or all of them can and probably will happen to a lot of prepared people after a catastrophic event.

So, what is the bottom line here? Keep what you have to yourself and within the family – this includes educating your children on not talking to others about what you have or are doing.

What You Can Do To Prepare

Knowing that there is a very good chance that what we have worked so hard to put away for ourselves and families, in time of an emergency disaster, could potentially get taken from us, is the first step in preparing to protect it.

Consider redundancy of your preps and store them away from your homestead or home. A creative way to accomplish this is to make caches or hidey-holes. For instance, by using an air-tight 6" PVC pipe you can make a container (a PVC pipe with end caps) to store some food and supplies in. Make the container(s) to whatever length you want. Drop them into a nearby lake or pond – with a string tied to them for retrieval – or place one down a hollowed out tree stump. Be creative. You can also hide things in plain sight. There are a lot of creative ways to hide, disguise, or conceal things. Like a fake picture frame to hide some money in. Or a decorative barrel that you can put supplies down in. Do your research. It is amazing how creative people are and the ideas you can get from them.

And lastly, you need to have a way to protect your goods. How you do this, and what you do it with, is entirely up to you and your unique situation, but this issue needs to be addressed, and done as an integral part of your survival strategy.

Remember, even, good people will do what it takes when their life or that of their family is at stake. You need to understand this and do what is necessary to assure the safety of you, family, and possessions. - Just sayin'.

Notes:

Cutting Off Sound:
Situation Awareness

Have you ever considered just how much noise we have around us? Think about it. You start your day off with that darn blaring alarm-clock. The cat and dog make their animal pleas for you to get up and get them some food. The automatic coffee-maker gurgling as it brews your liquid energy. And, water from the shower splats as it attempts to beat the sleepiness out of you. All in the first 15 minutes of your day!

Then, as you rummage through your clothes closet, thrusting hangers to and fro as they clank in to each other, clothes being tossed about like a Kleenex in a hurricane as you decide on something to wear. Once you decided on your wears of the day, you shuffle down the hall to the kitchen; bunny slippers snapping in time, as you grab a bowl from the cabinet, slamming the door with your shoulder; pour a cup of coffee and plunk a clean spoon retrieved from the dish drain into the bowl. Next, you grab the box on the counter; left there from your late night snack, and open the cardboard flaps, uncrinkle the waxy bag to pour your favorite *nuttin' but sugar* cereal. Plopping down on the sofa with a thud, you cross your legs Indian-style, turn on the television set and, listen as your trusty news anchor tells you what you can expect for your daily commute. Finishing your cereal and coffee, you pause for a moment to listen to the perky weather girl tell you why that wool sweater you chose to wear wasn't such a good choice after all, before rising to go do your hair and make-up.

As the hair dryer screams, you turn on the radio – loud to hear over the hairdryer – and with one hand you attempt to respond to a text or two from your friends, and with the other dry your hair. Suddenly you see movement out of the corner of your eye. As you look up, there standing in your bedroom doorway is a bad guy, holding a gun. Panicked, your mind reels wondering how this person could have possibly gotten into your house without you hearing him. The answer is noise.

Noise is a distraction, and tuning it out takes practice. Our auditory system - ears to brain, doesn't work in harmony as well as say, our eyes to brain. In fact, our auditory system finds it difficult to separate noise from information. Noise can consume so much brain function that it makes it impossible to think about what is going on around you. Have you ever heard someone say, "Shut that radio off I can't think straight?"

An intruder not only made it into the house, but down the hall, and to the bedroom without being detected. That's a scary thought. We need to understand that we no longer live in a world where you can leave your doors unlock or your windows open. In order to protect ourselves we must develop better situational awareness. For those not familiar with the concept of *situational awareness*, it is the act of being aware of what is happening around us, and understanding how information, events, and our own actions can impact our goals and objectives. *Huh?* Okay, how about this then? It is being aware of our surroundings, sight, sound, smell – well all of our senses. Knowing what is happening around us, by using our senses, we can react accordingly. And, just as we do with other skills when practicing our survival preps, we must practice situational awareness as well.

What You Can Do To Prepare

How do we reduce the noise in our life? First, we might want to consider not texting all the time. Ouch! (I know.) But what does texting have to do with noise? Think about it. How are we alerted to a text? We hear a little chime or buzz, right? Then, almost instantly our heads jerk down as if by magnetic pull, our eyes scan the screen like a speed reader and our thumbs begin to jump around on the keyboard like a person feeling around for something in the dark – all the while we are oblivious to what is going on, around us. *That* is what texting has to do with noise.

Next, if you can't hear your radio or television at a normal level while doing other things, then turn it off. It only serves as a distraction. Learn to know what noises and sounds are normal to your surroundings, and what are not; again this is a practiced skill, like immediately recognizing the sound of the alarm clock buzzing or coffee brewing in the coffee maker, but not that thump you heard outside in the backyard, or the neighbor's usually quiet barking dog, or your cat jumping up on the window sill with its ears perked. All signs and sounds that should alert you that there may be a threat outside.

Learn to cut noise in your life out so that you are more aware of what is happening around you. Situational awareness will be a major survival skill if and when the poo-hits-the-fan. So, learn it and practice it often.

Shhhh!!! What was that noise? Just kidding – I wanted to see if you were listening. - Just sayin'.

When People Do Unspeakable Things
And they Will

In 1609-1610, Colonial Jamestown experienced a severe drought and subsequent famine that totally wiped out the community's food supply; in 1727 the English ship, the Luxborough Galley sank after catching fire leaving survivors afloat for two weeks in the mid-Atlantic; in 1820, the Essex, an American whale ship, was sunk by a sperm whale in the Pacific Ocean leaving its survivors afloat; in 1846–47, eighty-seven American pioneers were trapped by snow in Sierra Nevada while attempting to reach California from Missouri; and, in 1972, forty-five people, including a rugby team and, friends and family, crashed into the Andes Mountains, ultimately leaving 16 survivors.

So what's up with the history lesson? Well, this history lesson goes beyond what you have read so far. All of these dates in history have something in common, survival. (Well duh?!) Hear me out. Most if not all, of the survivors mentioned here were good, honest, upstanding, law-abiding people. The kind of people you would meet at church, at the grocery store, at a social event or just in passing. But, they were also ... cannibals (crickets).

In each of these tragedies, the survivors ate the dead to survive. "*Ugh!!!* I could never do that!" So you say, and I am sure these people would have said the same thing, before disaster struck.

In a catastrophic event, where food and water becomes a scarcity, if enough time passes, people will become desperate. This desperation will soon turn to survival of the fittest, which could mean doing whatever it took to feed themselves and families by whatever means. For these survivors, it was doing the unimaginable, eating another human being.

Let's take a closer look at what happened in Colonial Jamestown. First, there was a disaster – a severe drought that resulted in a famine. Famine equals no food. But, these people didn't just go out and start taking lives, when all their food supplies were exhausted, they did what they were most accustomed to doing, they hunted. Granted it was not their normal fare. They caught cats, dogs, mice, and snakes and ate them. Then, moved on to boiling their shoe and boot leather and ate that.

All in all, these things sound pretty disgusting. But as *real* desperation set in – they did what they had to do to survive, they ate dead corpses. When people have a *will* to live they will find a *way* to survive. Cannibalism was a way for these survivors to survive.

Imagine if there was an economic collapse, an EMP (atmospheric or nuclear) or any other disaster natural or man-made that would reduce or dry up our food supplies. When desperation sets in for us, will we be forced to hold on to deep-dark secrets too? Will we, like those in Colonial Jameson when faced with starvation move to more drastic measures? Will we begin looting, stealing from one another? Will we eat things never imagined, like a cat, dog, or a horse? Will we move on to eating insects and tree bark? What will we do when we've exhausted all those resources?

What You Can Do To Prepare

Why would I even bring up such a horrible topic? Because we need to be aware that these things have happened in the past and you can bet in a moment of desperation and starvation … it will surely happen again … and not just by bad people. As time goes on, people will revert back to a primal state – hunter/gathers to find food wherever, however possible, after a catastrophic event.

We have all experienced a hunger pang or two, after skipping breakfast, lunch or dinner, right? But have you ever gone days without eating? Or for simplicity sake, let's say *a day* without food? It's not a pleasant feeling is it? What about weeks without food? Now add to hunger pangs the stress of protecting yourself, your family and homestead and the anxiety of hunt or be hunted.

Without food our thinking will become muddled. Morals and values fly out the window. Soon you find yourself eyeing your sweet neighbor, Mrs. Reynolds, across the street, sitting next to her living room window – dead from starvation, and wondering if you can get to her before someone else does.

People say they don't believe in zombies … maybe they should reexamine that thought. Oh, good afternoon, Mr. Jones! Those are some nice looking legs you have there! - Just sayin'.

Notes:

What Weapon?
When Your Firearm Is Taken Away From You

I was asked by someone, what weapons could be used if we were to run out of ammunition or our firearm was taken from us after a disaster. Well far be it from me to even think I could come up with all the answers there are out there for this question, but I must say it did pique my curiosity. To be honest, when I heard this question, I thought, "Ya know, we really need to get away from the notion that if you don't have a firearm/gun you don't have protection. I mean, think about it. A weapon is any object that can be used to protect or defend ourselves, right? So that means A-N-Y-T-H-I-N-G can be a weapon!

If you have ever watched some of the old '60s television shows, you know the kind where the scorned woman hurls a lamp halfway across the room at someone? Voila! The lamp became a weapon. Well, more like a flying projectile. The problem with this scenario is that unless you're an Olympic weight lifter or have arms like some prize-fighter you are not going to have enough force behind you to do any real harm – well less smashing your favorite lamp into a bazillion pieces.

So my hunt was on - what could we use instead of firearms to protect ourselves? What did cavemen use? They used sticks and stones, even bones. Can't get any simpler than that! And, they were fighting things a whole lot bigger than what we will ever face in our lifetime (hopefully!) It just goes back to *anything* can be used a weapon with enough force.

Then I thought about the Bible character, David of "David and Goliath." What did David use? A sling shot and small stones. Again, David was up against something … er, someone who was way bigger than he was. Heck, David could have used a pea-shooter for that matter because it was all in the aim. The unprotected part of Goliath's forehead.

Think Indians. They used a bow and arrows for hunting and protection. You can buy or even make one. And, yes it can do great bodily harm.

Some of the traditional martial arts weapons of today actually came about when Asian farmers had their weapons taken away or banned, and began to use their farm tools; such as sickles, grinding sticks and staff for protection.

Look around your home and garage. There are tons of items everywhere, from the ink pen lying on the kitchen table, to the wasp spray in the cabinet, to the shovel in the utility room; all of these things can be used to defend you.

What You Can Do To Prepare

Now that we realize that anything can be used as a weapon, our next focus should be on where to aim that weapon. There are certain *sweet spots* or *vulnerable spots* on everyone. These are the areas that can cause the most damage, discomfort and yes, even death. We know a lot of the common *areas*, but here are some less common areas that you may want to keep in mind. There's the bridge of the nose (right between the eyes), above the ear, the philtrum (who knew the groove at the bottom of your nose to your upper lip had a name?), the chin, and in the Adam's apple (that weird protruding *knot* that guys have on the front of their neck). And while we are on soft targets, think about this, if a bad guy no longer has sight in his eyes after you jammed your thumbs in them, he really wouldn't be that much of a threat to you, now would he? Your hands, fingers, legs, feet can all be used to defend yourself. Or if the bad guy is bent over *taking care of business* from a punch to the groin you just gave him, it would allow you time to get out of harm's way or even administer a timely blow to his vulnerable unprotected noggin on your way out.

At home, we could defend ourselves by strategically placing deterrents around our property to ensure that we keep our home as safe as possible and, the bad guys as far away as possible. Think about creating landscape-type defenses; such as planting thistle bushes or blackberry bushes around the perimeter; both have menacing thorns that can deter even the toughest of bad guys.

You see, there are no right answers for what weapon we could turn to if our firearm, or weapon of choice has been taken or if we run out of ammunition. We should, however, have a backup plan and alternatives. As the preparedness saying goes, *"two is one and one is none."*

With any weapon, your focus should be on aim and force. Think like little David up against big Goliath and aim for that *sweet spot* – *thrappp* right between the eyes! - Just sayin'.

Got A Dollar?
Cheap Home Security Ideas

In today's economy for some, money has become something of a deterrent for properly protecting our homes. Most of us aren't able to afford those big elaborate home security systems, with glass breaking sensors, motion detectors, motion sensors, strobe lights, and loud alarms. But we can afford a roll of tape, right? A simple roll of tape along with some other household items can be the start to protecting your home. And most, if not all of these items, can be purchased at a dollar-type store.

With money as a primary reason for not properly protecting our homes, I began to wonder just how many inexpensive items we could use to protect our homes. My quest was on. I found a lot of items that could be purchased for a dollar each or even gotten for free. Remember I mentioned tape? Well that and fishing line or sewing thread are things we may already have handy. I'll get to how to use these things in a second.

Go out to your garage, up in the attic or in the basement. Look around. See any 2" x 4" pieces of wood lying around? If your door opens to the inside, you can use a 2" x 4" piece of wood as a wooden door jamb by placing the wood up under the doorknob to avoid the door being kicked open. Make sure the wood is at least three to six inches longer than the height of the doorknob. If you have access to a saw, cut a "V-shape" into one end of the wood so you can slip the notch under the doorknob. Then kick the bottom portion of the wood in towards the door for snug fit.

How about craft or hobby supplies? Do you have a thick wooden dowel (one inch or wider in diameter)? Place a craft dowel into the track of a sliding door to preventing it from being opened (a 2" x 4" piece of wood cut to length can also be used.) And, by backing out a few of the screws from along the top track of a sliding glass door you can prevent someone from being able to take a door off the track. A cheap fix, huh? And, free!

You can also use a dowel or piece of wood with sliding-type windows; up and side sliding. Place the dowel or wood piece above or to the side of the window to keep it from being opening from the outside (to have the wood blend in paint it the color of the window frame.)

Now, look through your holiday crafts. See those jingle bells? Tie a few bells together on a string and hang them on the doorknobs of the front and back doors to your house. Every time the door or doorknob moves - the bells will jingle. How easy is that?!

Now to the roll of tape, say you are going away for the weekend or on vacation, take some neutral colored thread; tan, grey, black, brown, or fishing line, and string it across the back gate of your home about 24" high, and tape the thread on either side of the gate-post. Then, do the same at the back door to your home; from the inside. When you arrive home from your trip; walk around to the back of the house, to see if the thread has been disturbed. If it has, then check the back door. If both lines have been broken, don't go into the house until you have contacted law enforcement.

Another tape idea is to make a security seal. The concept is like those labels fastened on items to avoid tampering with. If going away from home, take a piece of clear tape and place it on the lower corner of all exterior doors on the side of the door that opens. When you return, if the tape has been pulled off, you know you might have had a visitor while you were gone. You can also use tape on your vehicle for security by putting it on your doors, hood and trunk while at work or in a parking lot – of course there might be an issue with tape residue in the hot Sun so keep this in mind.

A business card will work much like the tape idea - an old detective trick. Put a light-colored card down in the corner of the door. If someone opens the door, the card drops out. Again free! People are always handing out their business cards!

Now, if you don't do anything else, at least do this one. Door frames are pretty flimsy, and bad guys know it. That is why they tend to kick a door in, opposed to risking injury by breaking a window. To remedy this, remove the tiny screws from the strike plate on the frame and replace them with a couple of 2" to 2 ½" wood screws. Screw the wood screws through the strike plate into the door framing and then into the housing frame. Then install a deadbolt that can also be purchased at a dollar-type store. So for $1.50 your door is secure.

These are just a few of the many security measures that cost little to nothing. Do some research on a problem area you may have. You just might be surprised that there is a cost-efficient way to remedy it.

What You Can Do To Prepare

Contrary to popular belief, security does not have to mean spending a lot of money to be safe. It can also be about being creative; like using the piece of wood under the doorknob idea. If you don't have any wood handy, and you happen to drive past a construction site, stop and ask if you can have a piece or two of scrape wood. More likely than not they are just going to cart the scraps off away so why not put them to good use. Or, the jingle bells on the doorknob idea? After the holiday sales practically give their decorations away. The bells won't cost a lot of money and yet they can work just as well as a bunch of loud obnoxious alarms going off.

Oh, one thing I didn't mention was a dog. Granted, a dollar-type store won't have dogs for sale, but I bet you can get one for free! And, a dog will afford instant companionship and the best security system money could buy ... if you had any, that is!! – Just sayin'.

Notes:

Why We Scream When We Are Frightened: Our Built-In Defense Mechanism

Some of us scream when we are frightened. Why? Well, for me at least, I'm usually concentrating on what I am doing or thinking about something at the time and therefore totally oblivious to what else is going on around me. So, if someone comes up behind me, beside me or in front of me … I scream; a loud, arduous ear-piercing scream. I could be brushing my teeth, washing my car or working on writing an article, but I'm thinking; concentrating on what I'm doing, and if someone or something happens to startle me … I scream. And, I mean really, really loud.

I hate when I involuntarily scream. I feel so stupid afterwards and turn into a babbling idiot as I try to explain why I screamed in the first place. I've even screamed when I was alone. Like the time a leaf dropped off a bush while I was busy working in the garden – or had a surprise visit from a frog. Thankfully no one was around at the time so I didn't have to explain my sudden outburst. So, why do I scream like that? I thought it worthy of looking into further especially if the poo-ever-hit the fan.

Screaming is a natural reaction. It's an internal defense mechanism – an automatic psychological process - that helps to protect us. It's inherent. We begin life screaming right out of our mother's womb and keep right on screaming throughout life.

Have you ever been around someone who screamed so loud it hurt your ears? (Two year olds are good at this.) A scream can generate up to 100-125 decibels of sound pressure – now compare that with normal conversation which is 60 decibels (no wonder those screams hurt our ears!)

So, I was thinking. We could use our scream as a distraction if threatened. If we screamed loud enough and right into a bad guy's ear, we could momentarily stun him. His natural instinct would be to blink, move his head, and pull away from the noise – our scream. As we scream, our stomach muscles tighten giving us that spurt of energy *and* a window of opportunity to cram our fingers into his eyes, ears, or nose, then push away and run! Caveat: you may only have this one opportunity, so make it count!

Now, this may sound a little funny, at least it did to me, but defensive screaming takes practice. It's another learned tactic. You begin your practice by taking a deep breath – deep as if you were pulling the air up from the bottom of your feet. Then, let the air out forcefully, in the form of a scream, from deep down in your stomach. As you do this, you will feel your stomach muscles tighten as oxygen courses through your body. The oxygen is what gives you that surge of power and keeps you alert. Oh, one other thing. I'm not sure where you are going to find a place to scream, I don't think there are any *screaming ranges* – so practice might be a little tricky.

What You Can Do To Prepare

When being confronted by a bad guy, he is focused on his objectives, and waiting to accomplishing his mission without being noticed or attention being drawn to him. It could be to harm you, steal your money, or your possessions … anything, he just wants to do it quickly and quietly, and get outta dodge. This is where screaming comes in to play as a defensive measure. Experts have said that screaming the word "fire" opposed to "rape or help" can give you a better chance of getting noticed and/or someone coming to your aide. The premise behind this is theory is that screaming "help or rape" frightens people and they don't want to get involved for fear of being hurt. But, screaming "fire" on the other hand, could involve them and their safety, so they are more apt to come to your aide.

The problem with the "help/fire" premise is that when we are under stress your innate emotional survival responses kick in automatically – think fight or flight. Sure, your intellectual responses *know* you should yell fire, but these responses will be overridden by your natural instinct for survival. So, although we know what we are supposed to do, we might want to forget words and just concentrate on using our naturally inherent defense mechanism called *screaming* – scream as loud and with as much intent as possible. Oh, preferably in an ear … the bad guy's ear.

Noise is an effective and proven deterrent. So scrreeamm!!! – Just sayin'.

Notes:

When Bad Guys Stop the Good Guys
Guns and Disasters

Bad-guys do bad things. That's why we call them "bad ... guys," right? But, during disasters these bad-guys have been known to kick it up a notch, and become even "badder" (it could be a word), by committing senseless acts of violence, against personal property and human life. These guys will kill for the sake of killing. They will steal for the sake of stealing. And, they will destroy for the sake of destroying. But why do they do it?

During *Hurricane Katrina*, as medical aid, doctors, nurses, and rescue teams flew in to help the citizens of New Orleans, sniper fire by well-armed bad guys, who were slowly taking over the city streets; raping and murdering innocent people along the way, fired on the helicopters. Again, we ask why? My guess, is because they could get away with it.

After the hurricane, bad-guys knew that the police would be busy with more pressing matters, such as evacuations, crowd control, and monitoring for looters, therefore wouldn't have the time or the man power to patrol the city streets properly. The bad-guys seized this window of opportunity for their advantage and began "taking matters into their own hands" by committing horrendous crimes.

Because of the actions of these bad guys, a lot of the rescue efforts halted for a time for fear of life or limb. And, I have to say, I can't blame the rescuers one bit, I mean, why risk being shot or injured while you are attempting to save others? Some of these rescuers; ordinary citizens like you and me, just trying to help-out.

What ultimately slowed the bad-guys down was 15,000 soldiers; ordered to restore the peace. Soldiers called-in for a disaster? Yep, 15,000 national guardsmen and air national guard were called-up to protect first responders – and citizens.

Unfortunately, with this calamity also came something that, in my humble opinion, should never have happened. Authorities ordered law-enforcement to enter homes of honest, law-abiding citizens (to the pleasure of the bad-guys I'm sure), and re-victimized them by confiscating the only means they had of protecting their homes, families and, what little belongings were left – their firearms. I'm sure when the authorities made their decision to remove weapons their thoughts were in the right direction – safety; even possibly thinking it would eliminate the violence. But it backfired. Instead, the citizens were left defenseless against the hordes of bad-guys still out on the streets and armed. One sweet older woman, whose home thankfully was not flooded or damaged, explained to officers who came to her home that she was fine, had enough food and water, and wished to stay put with her dogs. Then, upon informing them that she also had a legal, unloaded firearm, the officers threw her to the ground and her gun was confiscated. I mean, really? Was that necessary? No, but it happened. That sweet older woman went from a nice woman caring for her dogs to a harden criminal in zero to sixty seconds!

Thankfully, out of all this tragedy, destruction and countless deaths – directly and indirectly - as a result of *Hurricane Katrina*, something good did come out of it. The "Disaster Recovery Personal Protection Act of 2006" bill was introduced in the United States Congress to prohibit the confiscation of legally possessed firearms during a disaster. These provisions ultimately became law in the form of the "Vitter Amendment to the Department Of Homeland Security Appropriations Act, 2007." Soon thereafter, several states followed suit with their own laws.

What You Can Do To Prepare

Legally having a firearm to protect yourself, family, belongings and property, is your right under the 2nd Amendment to the Constitution. It could likewise be the difference between being a victim or a citizen protecting their home and family. Having a firearm is the surest way of confronting a criminal. (Caveat: you have to be determined to not be a victim and willing to actually use the firearm.)

Think about this. During a disaster where authorities are busy protecting citizens and properties; no one is manning the jailhouse. So, let's say these inmates find their way out of the jailhouse with the help of their bad-guy friends. You now have inmates and bad-guys out on the street, most of them armed.

The point here is this, there have been many stories told after disasters; that when faced with a firearm by honest, law-abiding citizens protecting what is theirs, bad-guys are deterred. Bad-guys usually take the easy road – why risk their life when there are so many other *easy-picking* targets out there? Deterrence works. Bad-guys don't want being shot anymore that we do.

So, am I telling you to get a firearm for protection during a state of emergency? No, that is a decision for you and you alone to make. But, what I am telling you, is that there are Federal, and in some cases state laws to protect you and your 2nd Amendment rights to have a firearm during a disaster; thereby affording protection to you, your family and personal property. What you do with this information is up to you. - Just sayin'.

Notes:

Let's Pretend:
Fire Drills for Survival

We tried an experiment at our homestead, a life-altering experiment. It was a real eye-opener for me. For a week, everything that we cooked, we cooked on our gas grill, and alternative cooking sources – outside in the heat, cold, and yes even the rain. This included breakfast, lunch and dinner; and anything in between. Now, we aren't talking *cook-out* meals like hamburgers and hot dogs – we are talking, every meal that I would normally cook or make on the stove or in the oven was fixed on the grill. Spaghetti, pizza, steak, chicken, potatoes, rice, veggies, and popcorn – anything I did on the stove top or oven I did on the grill. I also washed all dishes, utensils, pots and pans and silverware by hand, in my outdoor sink, using only water from our rain catchment barrels; boiled on the gas stove, and left them to air dry.

We bathed with soap and a washcloth; me from water heated on the grill and then poured into a large bowl, and hubby using a solar shower bag hung out during the day to heat up. For hair washing days for me, I washed my hair first and then bathed.

No electricity of any kind was used during this week. Instead, we used solar lights (outdoor garden solar lanterns), that we kept out in the Sun during the day, and brought them in at night to disperse throughout the house. (It's amazing how little light you actually need.)

The toughie for me, I must say (you're probably thinking bathing and hair), was pulling out the never-before-used port-a-potty we made (this was before I invented the *Hiney*

Hydrant™), but I knew going in that this experiment it wasn't gonna be fun. I placed a scented bathroom trash can bag in the potty (consisting of a 5 gallon bucket and a portable toilet seat and cover), did my business, then poured a little multi-cat clumping cat litter in the trash bag (I figured, it was odor eliminating and, if it is good enough for cat *wee-wee* and a house full of cats then it should surely work for this purpose too!) I tied the bag and placed it into another lined bucket with a lid – kinda like a diaper pail sans the baby. Although it wasn't the most pleasant of things … it worked.

So what did I learned from this experience? Well one thing, if the world as we know it was to come to an end today, a lot of us would be in big trouble. What we did was hard, time-consuming, and downright inconvenient. Everything required thought. But, in order to see what we might be up against, and the areas that needed improvement, we had to do this if we want to really survive.

What You Can Do To Prepare

I'd like to challenge everyone to do this experiment – if only for the weekend. Include your family members and/or friends – even the ones that you know may come knocking at your door should the poo hit the fan.

Keep in mind what I said, this will be hard, it will be uncomfortable and a lot of work … "a lot" of work. Soon, you will notice others, and you, becoming irritable, angry, tired, frustrated – the gamut of emotions. And this is *practice* for what could be *the real thing* one day.

Most of you, as human nature usually dictates, will probably cheat. If you do, just keep in mind - you will only be cheating yourself. If a disaster should happen and you are forced to leave your home, you may find yourself doing these same things, and more - only this time you can't cheat. – Just sayin'.

Notes:

Three Is Company:
Survival Rule of Threes

You have three minutes to live or die! Did you know that there are actually rules to survival? In a wilderness survival situation, it is important that you are aware of what your body is capable of – and hopefully, after reading this, you will never have to find out the hard way.

Remember these rules of survival; known as the *Rule of Threes*, to understand where to put your priorities in a survival situation. They are in order:

You can survive 3 minutes without oxygen;

You can survive 3 hours without shelter;

You can survive 3 days without water; and,

You can survive 3 weeks without food.

Can you imagine three weeks without food? I would have guessed three days, but three weeks is a very long time. *Geeze*, three hours for me is a very long time sometimes.

Have you ever gone down a long water slide, hit the water hard, and dunked under the water? The less than ten seconds seems like a long time without air – let alone three minutes.

These rules are for guidance and don't apply to every person exactly the same way in every situation. I mean, we all are a little different from one another. Some of us are big, some small, some have more *protection* around us, and some don't have enough. We're all different. Some of us can work right through lunch and not miss a beat while others are hungry just a few hours after breakfast.

When faced with a wilderness survival emergency, the one mistake that most people seem to make over and over is that they put food as their top priority. (Remember, food hunger is the one thing that we can last the longest; three weeks.) So, even though you may hear and feel growling hunger pangs coming from your stomach, you need to focus more on shelter and then water.

Our bodies are remarkable machines and are actually built for survival. Making a shelter is your top priority because you need to have a warm, dry, covered area to rest in. One of the easiest ways to make a shelter is to take dry leaves or pine needles and make a really big pile. Then, just like you did when you were a kid (well some of us did), burrow yourself into the pile of leaves. You can also use pine needles to make a dry ground layer for insulation from the ground if you already have something you could cover up with.

As for water, while it is true your body can go three days without water, you will probably start to feel the effects of dehydration after only 12 hours or so. Our bodies are made-up of mostly water and without it we may not be able to think as clearly. One way to seek water is to watch for animals and, if safe to do so, follow them and/or their tracks (be careful to know what animal you are actually following before doing so!) Also, watch or listen for birds as they tend to congregate around water as well.

Condensation is another way to get water. Dew droplets (not to be confused with *doo droplets*), will build-up on leaves and create beads of water. By carefully pouring each leaf into one central leaf you may have enough water to hydrate yourself until you can find a better water source.

The climate also has a lot to do with these rules. For instance, if you are in a hot climate, three days without water could be shortened greatly, especially if you sweat a lot.

Now let's move on to the subject of food. It is only after you have taken care of the first needs; shelter and water that you should begin to look for food. Within the food rule there are other rules, unofficial rules, such as, stay away from mushrooms – period, there are just too many poisonous mushrooms to know the difference between the safe ones and poisonous ones. To make food hunting a little easier, here's a good way to remember some forest food choices: if it walks, swims, or crawls (unless it is brightly colored), you are probably good to go. Small animals, fish and insects are your best bet (*yum.*). If small game is not your cuisine of choice, maybe insects are? Just don't eat anything that has more than six legs. Oh, and all fur-bearing animals are edible, as are all birds – the skinning, degutting and plucking are a little burdensome, but the reward of meat will only make it taste that much better (or so they say).

What You Can Do To Prepare

A lot of people consider the "Rule of Threes" to apply only to wilderness survival, and yet there have been countless stories of how these same rules played a critical part in the survival of people involved in natural, man-made, or other disasters.

If you ever find yourself in an extreme situation where it could be the difference between life or death, prioritizing your survival needs will be your primary goal. Knowing the "Rule of Threes" will help you accomplish this goal.

Oh, and something else, it has been said that you can only survive three months without human contact and/or hope. Hope may be a little easier to come by if perhaps you started out with a positive outlook and optimistic attitude before the emergency event. Companionship, on the other hand, hmm, well, you might wanna start looking for volleyball. *"Willlll-son!"* ... (A reference to the movie *Castaway*) - Just sayin'.

Notes:

Hey Joe, Is That You?
How Women Can Disguise Themselves to Look Like a Guy

Do you ever think about your safety being compromised in a poo-hits-the-fan scenario because you are a woman? I mean, let's say we had to get to our safe destination fast, and for some unforeseen reason we were not able to get to our vehicle or back home, and had to start hoofing it on foot … alone (hopefully with some form of survival supplies in tow – or if nothing else a pocket multi-tool). Note: disasters know no time – so it is important that we have a go-bag in multiple locations; work, home, vehicle or even a relative's home, et cetera.

So, here we are in the midst of a bazillion refugees (the dreaded "Golden Horde") – a female, walking alone. What do you think the chances are that we would be singled out sooner or later because we are female? You know, like a predator stalks a weaker prey picking them off one by one? Or taking advantage of an opportunity … us? If we were guys, would it make any difference? Well, maybe.

This is a scary thought and it got me to thinking. What if we could disguise ourselves to look like a guy? You know, get in touch with our inner "masculine side"? I think we could do pretty well with the disguise part. But *acting* like a guy? *Hmm.* That just goes against the very grain of who we are, doesn't it?

Like I said, the clothes would be easy. Jeans, t-shirt, flannel shirt or hoodie, boots or sneakers, a belt and ball cap or knit cap and we're good to go. How about the mannerisms, how do guys act? Well, I did a little researching on guy-habits, and found they all don't act the same - just like all women don't all act the same. Which, I guess actually could work in a woman's our favor in this case.

I think the closest thing we as women do to imitate a guy, is we talk in that weird deep-throaty-voice when we describe what a man said. Like for instance, you tell a friend, "My dad said, (interject weird deep-throaty voice) "You had better be home by 10." But, I think for our safety, in a situation where our life could be in danger, this is something that we really may want to think about a little more seriously and, approach it like any other survival tools and plan. Again, let me stress this is not how all guys act (so guys if you are reading this don't get all weirded out, okay?) This is just a guideline to go by.

Now to what I found, guys tend to make loud noises (I know *ewww!*) and not excuse themselves for any of them. That goes for burps, farts, grunting, throat clearing, spitting, snorting, slurping and hocking loogies- to name a few. Then there is the crotch thing; scratching, grabbing, pulling and that *rearranging thing* they do, okay, I'll stop there. Also, guys tend to talk loud and at times with a mouth full of food (I'm not trying to be disgusting just factual.)

There you have it "guy mannerisms 101." The best way, in my opinion, to imitate a guy is to think everything we are not and merge these things in with our disguise.

What You Can Do To Prepare

I never really gave much thought to disguising myself for safety reasons, let alone disguising myself as a guy. But, when you think about it, if we were in a crowd of refugees and all alone; no family or friends, and we saw a big group of rowdy guys approaching us from behind, I would think that we would want to blend-in as much as possible, opposed to standing out or being singled out? So, as a suggestion, you might want to try some of the guy mannerisms even if it's just in the privacy of your own home; in fact, yeah, I think you would want to do this in the privacy of your home opposed to going out in public and doing it. I mean, as it is, you are probably going to get a lot of weird looks from your family and friends when you grab your crotch and begin burping, farting, grunting, clearing your throat, spitting, snorting, slurping, hocking loogies – and talking in that *weird deep-throaty voice*. But then, maybe not as weird as when you tell them you are practicing your survival skills!

Just a thought, and maybe a better solution, you could practice your *man-skills* at a costume party? Dress up like a guy and see if you can actually pass yourself off as one – if it works you know you have another sure-fire survival tool. So get to practicing Mr. Man! – Just sayin'.

Notes:

✌ 4 ✌

Survival Mindset

To All the Moms - Who Got It Before We Did

My mother was the oldest of seven kids; which meant she had to help raise her younger brothers and sisters while her parents worked. She did the cooking, cleaning, washing of clothes – and all while still finding time to go to school (walking five miles; *really*), her homework and somewhere in there, to rest. Due to her upbringing, my mom swore when she had kids that they would not have to endure the lifestyle she had. And, we didn't. No cooking, no cleaning (okay I had to do a little dusting here and there), no domestic duties at all. Instead, my siblings and I focused on all-things-social. If there was a club, I wanted to belong to it. A dance, I wanted to go. And, if there was a sporting event, *oooh-weee*, I was there. Not for the sports mind you, but for the people and food!

In my consumer mindset world, I survived well. When in doubt I bought it … which meant; maid service to dining out. I'm sure this all sounds glorious. But the truth of the matter is it has been a major prepping hurdle. Why? Because I didn't learn to cook, bake, how to tell if a fruit or vegetable was ripe, what I should pay for something at the grocery store, like a pound of hamburger – how to use cooking measurements, or even how to keep a plant alive.

Not knowing how to do many of the things I mention, was the main reason I chose to move closer to my parents, as part of my preparedness plan. I wanted to learn how by mom did things during hard times, and how she did them now. And, who better to learn from? Right?

My hubby and I made the move and I dealt with the withdrawals of not having a shopping mall on every corner (the closest thing to shopping here is a Walmart and that is about 45 minutes away.)

As I shared my thoughts with my mom, on the economy, EMPs, disasters, politics ... you name it, I wasn't always sure she really understood the *preparedness thing*. She knew what it was like not have a lot, and how to make do with what you have. She always had a lot of canned goods, a nice garden, water, a back-up generator, blankets, and emergency lighting. But, for her these things were for that *just in case* time when they lost power from a storm – not ... prepping, or whatever I was *calling* what I was doing.

I loved talking to my mom and asking questions about the difficult times that she and her family went through and how they "survived". So many 'little nuggets' were learned during those talks.

For nine glorious months I watched as my mother cooked and baked; taking mental notes, and asking questions along the way. She cooked like she did many things, "by feel" from years of doing them. I must admit, at times, this was a little frustrating because I wanted to know exactly how she knew how much to add of this and that when she was making something. Her response was always the same – just add until it looks right or tastes right ... or (fill in the blank) right. And my response was usually the same too, "Yeah right."

Then, one Sunny morning, a man late for an appointment ran a stop sign going 55 mph, at the exact same time my parents were crossing the intersection driving into town. The driver broadsided the driver side of my parents' car killing my dad instantly. Their car was then shoved across the street and into a telephone pole, killing my mother as well. It was the first time in the nine months since moving that I was not driving my parents to town; I had a prior appointment that day.

In that split second all the knowledge I had hoped to gain and both of my parents were gone.

What You Can Do To Prepare

I share all of this to say, our parents and grandparent are a wealth of information. If still living, or if you have senior neighbors, family members, or even friends at church, we need to talk to them and try to learn as much as possible from them about how they once did things. Who better to know then someone who has lived it, right?

My mission and goal, as a lot of you know, is to share as much as I can with everyone and anyone about how to better be prepared should a disaster of any kind strike. I do this in honor of two of the most giving people I know, my parents.

Oh, and just as a side note, when going through my mother's belongings after her death ... there sitting right inside her bedroom closet, was a small backpack – and in it? She had all kinds of prepping things. It was her emergency go-bag. Apparently she *did* understand what I was saying after all.

Miss and love you and dad so much, mom! - Just sayin'.

And One to Spare:
Having Enough to Barter

If and when the poo ever hits the fan we may find ourselves in a world where money no longer has a value (as if it does now, right?). If this happens, we may need to barter (trade) with others for goods (food, gear, supplies, et cetera.) or services (chopping wood, cooking, sewing, harvesting, you know, all-thing-manual).

To anticipate this world, as part of our preparedness plan, we may want to consider creating a little *barter stash* — items over and above our own survival basics of food, water, medical supplies, and means for protection and self-defense.

After the poo hits the fan, there will be a lot of people, let me stress, "a lot," who are not as prepared as us, or not prepared at all. And, yet some of these people just might have something we need ... perhaps knowledge or a skill-set that we don't know how to do or are not physically capable of doing.

The thought process behind bartering is that if we had a few extra well-planned items, we could trade some of these items in exchange for something we may need, or for the help of someone to get something done that we may not otherwise be able to do, or like I mentioned, not physically capable of doing; or doing well.

We have to be very careful and cautious about our transactions - making sure not to disclose too much – or all of our "extras" to anyone. Keep in mind, loose lips sink ships ... the ship being you.

A good way to start your bartering stash is to pick up extras like rice, beans, pasta, flour, sugar and powdered milk ... you know the staples. Then, begin to think of all the different things that someone could need if displaced. It could be cooking supplies, such as pots and pans, utensils, plates and cups; a way to stay warm; so socks, matches, blankets, knit-hats, scarves, gloves and tarps; a way to repair things; like maybe a needle and thread, duct tape, super glue, safety pins, buttons, and scissors; and even garden items; like a shovel, rake, work gloves, seeds. There are so many things that we could barter with. If someone was sick or not feeling well, you could barter medicines like, aspirin, antibiotics, antihistamines, histamines, laxatives, antacids. Even the most prepared of people don't always think about medications. Who plans for heartburn? Am I right?

Books are also another item that could be invaluable and great to barter with as well. Think about it, if we were left without power; which would mean for most, no computers or devises to research anything, we would need to look up things the old-fashioned way ... yep, books. Start looking for "how-to" books – which, by the way, you can find fairly cheap at "used books" stores and yard sales, on topics such as home improvement, building, plumbing, gardening, cooking, camping, and first-aid would all be great books to have. Heck any "how-to" books would be!

Think about this too. We are all going to get dirty, very dirty. So cleaning and grooming supplies, laundry detergent, and soaps (liquid and bars) are a huge plus too. We may have to haul our water, but at least we'll have items to clean ourselves up with after all that sweating. Just think what a bar of soap would mean to someone who hasn't bathed in a while? Sounds like heaven right?

As for ammunition for bartering, I'm not even going to go there because frankly it is way beyond my knowledge base. So, it's up to you if you want to include it. Just keep in mind that this could open a whole can of worms you might not want opened by letting others know you are a person who has weapons ... and ammunition to go with them. I would personally steer away from guns and ammunition for bartering and just stay with "wants and needs."

What You Can Do To Prepare

Bartering is not just about things – goods. It is also about skills and knowledge, or services. Everyone has a skill or two; we just may not use them that often. For example, have you ever mentioned that you did something and were then met with the response "I didn't know you could do that"? After the poo hits the fan, everyone will be dusting off their skills, and knowledge – with, or without supplies. So, keep this in mind, just because you have a storage room packed from floor to ceiling with preparedness supplies and gear, it doesn't mean you know how to use all that stuff ... but somebody may and will be eager to trade. – Just sayin'.

Notes:

Prepping:
Real Life Insurance

There are so many predictions circulating out there, and by so many people – Bible scholars, psychics, economists, conspiracy theorists – regarding if and when a real catastrophic "poo-hits-the-fan" event will occur. You know the kind, like the sky is falling, flooding of biblical proportions, inferno fires, streaking comets out of the sky, and the next great depression? I don't have a clue if or when anything of that magnitude will ever happen. But what I do know is that disasters do happen, and therefore, I plan on being prepared for anything that comes my way. I choose to error on the side of caution, by having "survival insurance."

We have auto insurance for when we have a traffic accident, home insurance for a fire or an act of God, and there are a bazillion other different types of insurance for whatever suits your fancy. So why not have insurance for your survival as well? Here's the caveat: It takes something other than money to get survival insurance.

The difference between survival insurance and other types of insurance is with survival insurance we gain it; it is not necessarily purchased in the true sense of the word. Think about it, we are a consumer mindset generation. It would be too easy to purchase survival insurance if it could be purchased. I mean after all, we buy items that do the work for us instead of us doing it. (For example, the automatic vacuum cleaner that vacuums the floor for us.) If this was the case, e-v-e-r-y-o-n-e would be a *prepper,* right? I can hear it now ... "Give me the best survival insurance you've got, - with lowest premiums and highest payouts." Yep! That's our world ... something for nothing!

Anything that matters, survival insurance included, takes work, not just money. What I mean by this is, with survival insurance we gain it with skills and knowledge. Skills such as gardening, making shelter and food gathering and preserving, water procurement, cooking, et cetera. Skills needed to help you survive a disaster or catastrophic event, and knowledge of how to do these things and apply them in different scenarios.

Just as with any insurance, the outcome unfortunately is not a given. There are no guarantees the outcome will be favorable. Even by having automobile insurance, you still might get injured in an accident. And, with survival skills, and knowledge, you may not survive a catastrophic event.

I am not a fortune-teller. And, probably neither are you. None of us really knows what the future will hold. But isn't that the idea behind prepping? Preparing for the unknown?

What You Can Do To Prepare

My suggestion is to create your own survival insurance by focusing on skills and knowledge opposed to "survival items," which could all be broken, lost, or taken. Skills, like knowledge, are in your head and cannot be taken from you. Like riding a bicycle, once learned, skills and knowledge are in our memory bank forever. The more skills we have, the more we can use them for our benefit and possibly the benefit of others as well. Read as much as you can. Take as many preparedness courses and listen to as many lectures as you can. Learn from other preparedness-minded people as much as you can. And then, practice your preparedness skills as much as you can. It's all up to you how much you gain.

Skills are learned and then perfected with practice and ultimately become our insurance. Just as they say, you can never have enough insurance; the truth of the matter is, you can never have enough skills and knowledge which equates to survival insurance.

Like I've always said, disasters and catastrophic events know no time. So while you are preparing for today ... you might want to think about preparing for tomorrow; just in case.

Hopefully tomorrow's disaster never comes. – Just sayin'.

Notes:

What Does Disaster and Catastrophe
Really Mean to You?

I was thinking ... I do that a lot, we use the words "disaster" and "catastrophe" quite a bid in our everyday conversation and probably don't even realize it. Case in point, how many times have we heard or even said ourselves, that (fill in the blank) was a total disaster? When in all actuality it was more like things just didn't go as planned or as we had hoped they would. Or, we describe something as a catastrophe, as in, "the cake was a catastrophe, when it was delivered one of the icing flowers fell off the top of it." Real Earth shattering huh? See what I'm talking about? On the other hand, when I use these words, I use them as catch-words to stress, well uncertainties; events that can happen that are totally out of our control; that could make a difference between living and dying. We seem to use these words a little more freely to describe occasions that are in no way related to a "life or death situation." When I say or write about disasters and catastrophes, they are exactly that; man-made or natural disasters, or topics and subjects that could cause a catastrophe such as the economy, social unrest, war and the threat of war; uncertain times. I try to stress that there is a greater chance than not that someone could be left to fend for themselves; if or when, these were to happen. Events that leave a huge question mark as to their outcome and that are usually out of our control, or cannot necessarily be predicted ... and could make a difference between surviving and not surviving a life altering event.

There are a lot of articles and books out there, for people who are already preparedness-minded that share little tidbits on how to better survive. That is not what I do. I talk about things that hit closer to home. My focus is on the people, who are just like I was, clueless to world events and the effect they could have on us. Writing is my way to share what I have learned about disasters and catastrophes, in hopes of helping another person or people, (with a special focus on garnering the attention of those high-heel clad girly girls), to understand what is happening in our world and how to prepare without having to give up who they are ... or shuck the dress and the handbag ... for camo and a tin hat.

What You Can Do To Prepare

One break, in the chain of life could mean the end of life as we know it. We can be prepared – for anything and everything – "if you prepare for one, you prepare for them all," as the saying goes. Let me be clear – I'm not saying we must live in fear – what I am saying is we have to be more aware of what is going on around us, and be prepared for whatever event; disaster or catastrophe, that may come our way. The *real* disasters. - Just sayin'.

Notes:

Why Barter Away Your Cannon When You Can Trade a Pea Shooter: The Art of Bartering

I don't drink alcohol. It's not by choice really – well yes it is. Let me explain. The reason I don't drink alcohol is because I am a light-weight. There I said it. My body just doesn't tolerate alcohol - period. I am the poster-child of a "cheap-date" for the drinking crowd. You know the one who downs a half a wine-cooler and they're up on the table swinging their napkin in the air, singing, and dancing away? That's me. (Sorry for that visual! I know, can't un-ring that bell!!)

So why am I even telling you all of this? Well, because the topic of bartering with alcohol came up in a conversation, and the question of whether you should even use alcohol to barter, and if so, should you trade a whole bottle verse a mini bottle. And … this got me to thinking about portions, and sizes of things that we would barter with.

A whole bottle of alcohol would be way too much for me. A mini bottle, however, would suit my "dancing on the table needs" just fine. And, as I thought about it, the same could hold true with a lot of our bartering items. Is a 50 pound bag of rice worth someone chopping wood for a fire for you? It would depend. Is this your last bag of rice? Is there any other way to get fire wood? Can you use some other alternative means for your fire? Is there a reason why you can't chop your own wood? Is this firewood for one fire or the winter? Do you have the means to replace the rice you just bartered? Do you even like rice? Does the person you are bartering with need 50 pounds of rice? See? There are many angles to look at when bartering.

If, or when the poo ever hits the fan, initially people will be desperate and therefore willing to barter anything and everything for … well anything and everything. But what if you knew the art of bartering? It sure would make things a little easier now wouldn't it?'

I first learned my bartering skills by going to yard/garage sales. At first, I cringed at the thought of going up to the person having the sale to ask if they would take something lower than what the item was priced. I just knew I'd be met with a harsh "No way!" response. But after trying it once or twice, I was usually pleasantly surprised by a "sure" and a smile. They had something I wanted and I had something they wanted. Bartering!

Before we go any further, for those who aren't sure what bartering is, it is a method of exchange. Trading items or services in exchanged for other items or services without using money (well except at garage sales.)

Bartering, also known as haggling, dickering, and trading, words than used to give me the heebie-jeebies, and conjured up images of backstreet dealings by shady characters. But, I got over it fast as I admired the (fill in the blank) that I got for next to nothing at a yard sale.

If you think about it, we've been bartering since childhood. Like when we traded a homemade cupcake for someone's chocolate bar at lunch in elementary school? You were sick of mom's cupcakes and loved milk-chocolate; the other kid's mom never had time to bake cupcakes and purchased all their snacks at the grocery store, it was a win-win situation for both. Then, we really got good at bartering in middle-school and high-school. We learned that food was also a way to get homework done. We would trade our chocolate chip cookies (an item) to a brainy classmate for help with our math homework (a skill) thus freeing up our time for more pressing matters ... our social calendars.

Now that we know what bartering is, how do we find the value of something? First, we need to look at the supply to demand ratio of the item. Huh? *Hmm*. Okay, remember the old song with the lyrics "I got a brand new pair of roller-skates you got a brand new key"? It's about someone having a pair of slip-on roller skates, but can't tighten them because they don't have a key. And, another person has a skate key, but no skates. Nope? Okay, bad example. How about this one? It is summertime and you have a bunch of socks to sell, but everyone is wearing flip-flops. There is not a demand for the socks in the summer, so the supply of socks is higher than the demand for them. You probably wouldn't sell very many socks, or if you did, it would be at a low selling price. Now, if you were to sell these same socks in the wintertime, the demand could be higher than the supply you have and you could actually increase the price a little more and still sell out of them.

Bartering is about needs. One person needs something for which another has. The other person has to decide if that person has anything they need to make a "fair" trade. Keep in mind that "fair" is subjective and it varies from person to person.

What You Can Do To Prepare

Think of bartering as another preparedness skill. And, as you would with other skills, practice them often so you are comfortable performing them. And, how can you practice bartering now? Does your lawn need cutting? Maybe you have sharpening tools inherited from your grandfather. You could barter with the lawn person to cut your lawn in exchange for them borrowing your sharpening tools to sharpen the blades of their lawnmower and other tools that they might otherwise have to pay someone to have done. It's that simple. You both have something of benefit.

Begin to open your eyes to opportunities for bartering. Make your approach with confidence. If you note someone who has something you need or has a skill that you could use – bring up the subject of bartering, you would be surprised at how many open-minded, and receptive people there are; especially in today's economy. During your bartering, watch the person's facial expressions and their body language or how they act during "negotiations," a lot is said through eyes and body movement. And, the worst that can happen is you can't make a deal and you walk away. No harm no foul.

It's almost a given, for some of us, bartering will become our way of acquiring supplies and items in the future as we deplete our preparedness food and supplies if the poo ever the hits the fan. Do some research now or get a book or two on bartering techniques. Oh, and don't just put your bartering books up on the shelf with all your other survival resource books. Read them … now. - Just sayin'.

How to Become a Rich Prepper

Everyone wants the American dream ... to be rich. Am I right? I mean who doesn't? Why else would there be all those *get-rich-quick* books, tapes seminars, and infomercials, on the topic? So, I got to thinking, "What exactly does being rich mean?" I mean, is it money? Is it stuff? You know, like a huge McMansion with fifteen bathrooms, or a private jet, or a garage full of rare exotic cars, or designer jewelry and clothes? (Eh ... excuse me while I wipe off the drool on my chin), or is it wealth in the form of dollars?

I like so many others, in the past, pursued that pie-in-the-sky dream. And, what did I have to show for it? A closet full of clothes, handbags and shoes – the good stuff mind you, but a lot of good all that stuff will do in an end-of-the-world-as-I-know it event!! I mean, right?

So how can we become a rich prepper? Well, if we look back in history (moan ... groan, I know, but hear me out), before there was money, (yes there was actually a time when money didn't grow on trees), items such as livestock, grains, herbs, spices, food, land and weapons were all used to "buy" from one another in the form of trading and bartering. It may have gone a little like this; "Hey I'll trade a chicken for some of your flour." sort of thing. Everything had a value. Then, along came precious metals; gold, silver, and platinum – and the cry ... "There's gold up in them-there hills!" In time, the precious metals were melted down and made into coins. (I guess it eliminated the need for a big wagon to pull all you precious metals around in) and, eventually became our currency.

These coins had a real value because of their content. Then someone came up with the brainy idea to collect these precious metals; gold and silver, and make a big ol' fort to store it all in. Which was followed with another hair-brained idea; probably made during one of the monthly Tuesday night poker games with the boys at the U.S. Department of Treasury in 1862 - because of a shortage of coins as a result of people hoarding them (remember these coins were made-up of gold and silver and had real value), and the need to finance the Civil War, they decided to make paper money. And, *ta-da*! We had what we now call money. Of course it is debatable about what, if any, the value our money actually has now, or will have in the future, based on what it is currently backed with — you know, air?

If our money doesn't have any real value now, or won't in the future, how can we become a rich prepper? We simply, we go full circle, we get rid of all our useless pieces of "stuff" that we have accumulated throughout the years — now stored in the abyss of your choice (attic, garage, basement, storage unit), collecting dust. And, by "get-rid-of," I mean sell it. Then, as you sell an item, buy something that will help you so you aren't so reliant on money (that's the point in this exercise mind you — get out of the habit of using money.) For instant if you sell that painting that has been wrapped-up in paper and sitting in the corner of your garage since your last move (12 years ago), sell it, and with the money buy seeds to grow a garden thereby cutting-down on the need to spend money for vegetables or herbs/spices later. Or, you could sell your water skis you haven't used in years, and use that money to buy self-protection and things that go along with self-protection (okay a firearm and some ammunition for protection.) Remember, one man's junk is another man's treasure, so really talk-up the item you are selling!

What You Can Do To Prepare

Scroll down your list of preparedness items to see what you still need; hopefully you have made a "wants and needs" preparedness list. If not, you might want to do this first. Then, as you sell something from your "I don't want or need this" stockpile, try to buy a needed item off your "wants and needs" list and then remove it from your list.

Soon, you will become that much closer to your goals of being self-sufficient, and not so reliant on paper currency, by using this system. And, if you do it right, in time, you will have gone full circle with history and once again be using items like grains, herbs/spices, food, and self-protection (okay firearms and ammunition) to buy from one another by trading and bartering. This is what will make you a *rich prepper* because as we know money will be worthless, and those who have relied on it will be "poo outta luck"! - Just sayin'.

Notes:

❧ 5 ❦
Health – Hygiene

The "Other" Flesh Eating Zombies

If the "get to a safe destination" part of your preparedness plan, your bug-out plan, or your need to leave your home quickly and quietly plan, includes stealthing through the backwoods of some dark forest, trampling undetected through a large grassy field, walking down an overgrown shoulder of a road, or rambling through the weedy banks of a river or lake - in the spring, summer or fall, to get to that "safe destination", you need to be aware of danger you might not know about. *Gulp!* (As if we don't have enough we will be focusing on already by steering clear of the refugees, looters and self-serving people, we now have yet another concern.)

I'm referring to the flesh eating grass zombies called *chiggers* who are just waiting to attack their juicy victims as they pass by. These zombies are so tiny that they are barely visible to the naked eye, but anyone who has experienced the wrath of these zombies can attest to the lingering misery they bestow – it really *is* beyond description.

Chiggers, unsuspectingly attach themselves to clothing from their perch on grass blades. Then, like someone wandering the food court at the shopping mall, they begin their destination to the most delicate (and I'm not using this word lightly), and thin skinned areas on a person's body; like the crotch and groin areas (that's where the delicate words come in), behind the knees, and in the armpits.

Chiggers don't just bite and leave like their cousins the mosquitoes (not really cousins – I just made that up); they inject a substance into our body (thus, their need for delicate, thin skin) – an enzyme, which ruptures our skin

132

cells. The skin around these injection sites then hardens and creates a straw-like opening; turning us into human sippy-cups so the zombies can slurp-up the fluids in our skin cells. *Ewwwwwww!* I know, right? And, the worst part is? Well, the next worst part. If somehow the chigger(s) go undetected, they can feed on our body for several days! Now that is a real *ewwwwww!!!!*

The good news is – believe me anything is good news after experiencing one of their bites, chiggers are usually detected and once they've eaten their meal they drop off or are knocked off. The bad news is (can it possibly get any worse?) we are left with a big red welt and unbearable itching caused by the sippy-cup straw left. Let me stress the *unbearable* part. One bite isn't so bad – well yes it is, but a colony of chiggers that have set-up camp around your "privates"?! Words can't describe it. And, worst yet, the itching can last up to two weeks! I am here to tell you that there is no lady-like or gentlemanly way to scratch those areas for relief in public!!

I say all this, to forewarn you, so you can start thinking of some sort of combat strategy to "aid" with the relief of an attack, i.e., the intense itching. This is where it gets tricky. Some people have notions that the chigger actually burrows itself under the skin and therefore, if we smoother it with some topical covering, it will kill the chigger and the itching will stop. Like applying clear nail polish to the welt, for instance, well they don't and it won't. Chiggers are just so tiny that you don't even know they were on you until you see the resulting "welt." What happens, when you apply nail polish to the bite (welt) is the air can't get to it and the itching stops ... temporarily. (For me, personally, I don't foresee me stopping to touch-up my nails when bugging-out, so it is highly unlikely that I will be stopping to re-polish my private parts either. Just sayin'.)

There are several remedies that people have used; with and without success, such as calamine lotion, corticosteroid creams, oral Benadryl, diaper rash ointment, *chiggerex* (a commercial product), mouthwash, toothpaste, rubbing alcohol, peroxide, oil, gasoline, bleach, and, baking soda, to name a few.

Some people have even been so desperate as to use a lighter and burning the bite, which to me is like hitting yourself in the head with a hammer because you have a headache! So I'd highly recommend against that one.

What You Can Do To Prepare

So, what have I used with success to relieve the itching caused by chigger bites? I have had good results with good ol' alcohol - not the drinking kind (although the itching could drive some to it), I'm referring to isopropyl rubbing alcohol. I just wipe the welts with the alcohol on a cotton ball and then let them air dry. Most over-the-counter remedies seem to relieve the itch to some degree – but it usually requires a reapplication periodically.

Now, speaking of itching, the only harm that comes from these little flesh-eating zombies is the itching – the real damage comes by us by scratching. Due to the unbearable itching we also scratch to relieve said itching. What happens is the bite can become infected and there lies the harm. I know, it's easier said than done, but try to avoid scratching as much as possible. (… yeah, I know, right?)

Okay, we know that chiggers will suck your will to live, but how do we avoid them in the first place? That is a toughie, because you can't really avoid them if you go outside in your yard or garden – chiggers are on just about every blade of grass – whole families of them. What I do is take garlic gel tabs – three of them, every morning during the fall, summer, and spring months, and that seems to work really well. It's not that I don't get bitten by these suckers, er ... sippers, because I do. But, apparently chiggers aren't big fans of Italian cuisine and so they usually won't continue on with the "tube and sucking my skin cell fluids" parts. I also tuck my pant legs into my boots and then stuff a dryer-sheet into the top of each boot before going out. I use the cheapest brand of dryer-sheet I can find; thankfully we don't have dryer-sheet-snob chiggers around here!! But the best thing I have found for avoiding the nasty bites of a chigger ... is to take off the clothes I have worn outside, when I come in for the day, and immediately take a shower. Remember we said those little critters can stay on us for days? You can knock them off, thus avoiding the dreaded "tube and sucking your skin cell fluid" thing by taking a shower.

How about if you are on the move? Here, are some suggestions for "trying to avoid" chiggers. Wear long pants and a long-sleeved shirt with thick socks and high shoes or boots. If you have any insect repellent, spray yourself down (such as DEET) this may help. Also, consider having a package of those wipie-sheets; like those *baby-wipes*, so you can wipe yourself down to help knock any latchers off, and avoid being their human buffet.

Oh and a FYI, scientifically speaking, chiggers are the larval form of the *common mite*. Thought you *might* wanna know that. - Just sayin'.

Notes:

No Way Am I Ever Giving Up Toilet Paper!
Famous Last Word

I haven't used toilet paper in years, honestly. And, I may never use it again … well here at home at least. I decided that I was not going to wait unit the poo hit the fan or any place else for that matter before securing an alternative to toilet paper. I just don't understand the concept of stockpiling toilet paper in your preps? It's not like food where we can replenish it from a garden. When it's gone – it's gone. End of story.

One of the many preparedness mantras I have adopted is always have backups for your backups. No exception. So it only seemed to reason that I would want to have backups for my back-end as well, right? I am a huge believer in cleanliness. Call me vain, call me a girly girl; just don't call to say you're out of toilet paper. Sorry Charlie!

When I began my search for toilet paper alternatives, I looked high and low, and there are a lot of things and methods out there – I mean, I'm amazed at what people are willing to use for alternative toilet paper! Can you honestly even imagine using corn cobs – the method of choice for our great-grandparents?

Let me share a little of what I found. I'll start with some outside bush craft-type methods first (you can tell this stuff came from wilderness guys.) Leaves; large, relatively green leaves from plants such as abutilon, hollyhocks, mullein, comfrey, wild grape, and mulberry are all said to make a good alternative to toilet paper. Uh, eh … really? Okay, I'm not trying to get gross here, but using leaves … doesn't that seem more like spreading, opposed to wiping off? Not good. Also, you need to make sure to avoid the scratchy or prickly varieties of leaves or you will have more issues than how to get clean. Then, there is snow. I'm not sure what the alternative will be for spring, summer and fall, but some say in the winter time to use snow to "clean" yourself (*brrrr*, I know). Make a small snowball about the size of your palm and form it into an oval-shaped and well ... okay, 'nuff said.

Moving inside the house we have the moist wipes ... but (no pun intended) in my opinion, this is the same as toilet paper, it takes up a lot of valuable space; sure not as much as cases and cases of toilet paper, but wipes will also run out. So moving on ...

There's the cloth or rag method. You cut up washcloths, old t-shirts or blankets into small squares to use. Once used, with cling-ons and all, you put the cloth in a pail of chlorinated water, only to have to deal with the poopy-floaties later (another *ewwww*, sprinkled with a *grosssss*.)

You can also use newspaper or phone books, like our grandparents also did ... but if you think we have a bad rap being called "hoarders" with our food stores and supplies, just wait 'til someone catches a glimpse of the stacks of newspapers and phone books.

Next, a portable water bidet, these are little plastic water bottles with a hook shape nozzle (similar to the size of a 16 ounce drinking bottle). You fill the bottle up with about a cup of water. To use it, you squeeze the bottle to produce a stream of water to cleanse yourself. The problem is, with most of these types of bottles, there is little to no pressure (the key to a good cleansing is pressure by the way) and one cup of water does not go a long way so you find yourself having to fill the bottle up a couple of times for proper cleansing. (Ever try to reach for something while sitting on the toilet?)

And finally, (this is really pretty gross), the left hand method where you wipe your hiney with your left hand (if you are right-handed that is – if left-handed, use your right hand) … no paper just your hand. And *that* my friend, to me is the mac-daddy of *grossness*! In fact, it reminds me of going to the zoo. There was always that one monkey that seemed to entertain young and old alike. You know the one - "Whoo Flung Poo"?

Still set on toilet paper? Let me share some interesting facts with you. Toilet paper has shrunk in size from 5" x 5" to 4.1" x 3.7". On average we use 8.6 sheets per trip to the potty – a total of 57 sheets per day. That my friends, is a lot of paper to stock up on!

What You Can Do To Prepare

So, what marvelous method did I come up with that I no longer use toilet paper? Well it was actually a means to an end … (giggle). I didn't invent this means to clean my end however. The item has been around for a long time. I just modified it to my liking.

The reveal … *drum roll please* – a simple one-gallon garden sprayer I purchased for $8. Wait … wait! Before saying anything, hear me out. I cut about 4 and a half inches off the wand to shorten it. I then placed the remaining wand (the part that connects to the water tank) in boiling water to soften it and shape it into a soft curve – a hook-shape – to make it gender friendly for those hard to reach areas due to obstacles for some of us. (I'm speaking about the men folks). Attach the wand back on the tank, and, *whaa-laa* a bidet with a control for a light summer mist to a full-on power blast. I call it the *Hiney-Hydrant*™

"But what about the wetness?" you ask. Well I purchased 18 white washcloths for $4 at Walmart and placed them in a container; folding them into each other like tissues in a Kleenex box. I then found a little flip-top trash can with a plastic bucket insert, and filled it 3/4 full with water and a homemade oxyclean-type cleaner (two parts water, one part hydrogen peroxide, one part washing soda.) When I do my business, I use the sprayer (bidet) and wipe dry with a cloth – with very little or next to nothing on the cloth. I then put the cloth in the bucket to soak. On laundry day, I empty the cloths and liquid into the washing machine add a little detergent and the cloths come out white as snow! (You don't have to do the wash cloths and bucket thing. I just like to keep things as sanitary as possible.) Oh, and I also spray the nozzle with a disinfectant after each use, just because.

The great thing about this little *Hiney-Hydrant*™ is that a gallon of water can last quite a while. And, the sprayer (bidet) sans the water is so light you can attach it to your emergency bag and empty a bottle of water into it when the need arises, pump it up and you're good to *go* (giggle.) So there you have it. How easy is that?!

Oh, and in paper's defense, as an alternative to your toilet paper, you could just wait for the devaluation of the dollar, and then use worthless paper money – I'm sure there will be plenty of it to go around for a long time – and if we need more, maybe we can get the Federal Reserve to print out some more. - Just sayin'.

Where'd Ya Get Those Pearly Whites?
Making Your Own Survival Toothpaste,
Whitener and Mouth Wash

I'll admit it; I'm pretty obsessed about keeping myself groomed; including my pearly whites. I just love the clean feeling of just-brushed teeth ... don't you? Did you know that most people actually look at your mouth when you are talking or when you first meet? And, what do they see? Yep, our teeth! Yikes! I have to tell you, knowing this has made me a little self-conscious at times, wondering if my teeth were as white or clean as they could be, especially after eating something. So, when considering all my personal grooming aids for my survival kit, and knowing that I may not have access to store-bought products if and when the poo ever hits the fan, I began to wonder what alternatives we would have for toothpaste.

During my quest to find the best alternative to toothpaste, I found all kinds of recipes, some good and some ... well not so feasible for an after the poo hits the fan scenario, so I decided to focus just on ingredients we may already have in our survival supplies, or if we didn't, it would be easy enough to add them, they are salt, baking-soda, and hydrogen peroxide.

By adding a little baking-soda and salt together in a small bowl, and then some water you can make a paste. Then, just dip your toothbrush in the paste and brush away! As an extra step, and to help combat gingivitis and periodontitis, gargle with a little 3% hydrogen peroxide afterwards, making sure not to swallow any. And, follow-up with flossing like you normally would do – or should. That's it!!

The reason baking-soda is so beneficial, is that it kills germs and bacteria in your mouth and removes plaque and stains on teeth. And, salt is rich in iodine and has great antibacterial properties and, helps neutralize acids in the mouth. Using 3% hydrogen peroxide helps with gum health, and that added benefit of teeth whitening. All three of these items are easy to use, effective, inexpensive, and easily transported. One small box of baking soda, a container of salt and a bottle of 3% hydrogen peroxide could last a while too.

Tooth decay is a serious issue in and of itself, but during an emergency disaster … it could actually become "a disaster within a disaster," so brushing will be even more crucial to do.

Now if you like whitening your teeth, like I do, here is an easy method. Strawberries! Yes, I said strawberries, those yummy red balls (well kinda) of sweetness that you grow in your garden. (If you aren't this would be a good reason to start.) Strawberries contain malic acid which acts as an astringent to remove surface discoloration. If you combine some of that baking soda you use for teeth cleaning and a strawberry it becomes a natural tooth-whitener, buffing away stains. How cool is that? Just take a ripe strawberry and using a fork, crush it to a pulp in a bowl. Add a ½ teaspoon of baking-soda and mix it with the pulp until it is well blended, and looks like a pink paste. Put some of the paste on a toothbrush and kinda spread the mixture on your teeth. Just like you would with commercial "whitening-type strips," leave the mixture on your teeth for about five minutes, and then brush thoroughly with your homemade toothpaste to remove the strawberry–baking soda mix. Then, rinse. And … here comes the floss again.

Strawberries have little seeds so make sure you floss after your whitening treatment to get rid of those little seeds that may get lodged between your teeth. Now here's the *disclaimer*: as with all good things, moderation is the key. This goes for teeth whiteners too. Be careful not to use the strawberry/baking soda whitening process too often. Strawberries contain acid which could damage the enamel on your teeth. *Not a good thing!* The common conscience is to not use the strawberry paste more than once a week.

Next, a bad breath remedy. Ever thought what you would do when you no longer have breath mints? Believe it or not … you can use parsley! The leaves of parsley are rich in chlorophyll and act as a powerful neutralizer for bad breath. So keep this in mind as you are woofing down those garlic knots with your favorite pasta meal, and then realize you have a social engagement to go to afterwards. To ward off the garlic, ask the waiter to bring you a few sprigs of parsley. Chew on them after dinner. And, as an added bonus, parsley when ingested helps reduce intestinal gases (*toot-toot*).

Now granted, garlic knots might not be a problem after an emergency disaster, but we will still, more likely than not, wake-up with "dragon breath." So, just like with the baking-soda and salt remedy for brushing teeth, the strawberry and baking-soda for teeth whitening, there is also a simple remedy for mouthwash. Boil some parsley and whole cloves together, let the mixture cool and then strain it. This makes a great mouthwash for that "oh so fresh survivor breath".

What You Can Do To Prepare

We have now seen that for less than we can buy most commercial brands of toothpaste, tooth whiteners and even mouthwashes, we can buy a box of baking-soda, a container of salt, a bottle of 3% hydrogen peroxide, pick a few strawberries and sprigs of parsley, and we will have our survival oral care covered. Now, smile pretty!!! - Just sayin'.

Notes:

Going Banana's Over Your Hair!

I admit it; I love all things hair and make-up. In fact, I am always on the hunt for creative ways to take care of my hair and body, soooo … when I read that bananas were great for repairing and conditioning your hair, I thought "Hmm, I wonder? And is my habit, I jumped on my computer and began to search for all the benefits of bananas and hair, to see if just maybe, bananas could be my deep conditioner of the future.

Now, let me say up front (as if you didn't already know), I am not a nutritionist, a chemist, an esthetician or a hairdresser, I am just me sharing what I have gathered from my research, so here goes. Bananas contain vitamins A, B, C, and E, and tryptophan (a rich amino acid) and potassium. They also are rich in natural oils and carbohydrates. No wonder we like eating them, right?! Well, good news so far! These vitamins and minerals are said to bring out the natural elasticity in our hair, make it super soft, and prevent split ends. Wow, that's sounding good isn't it? Bananas are also supposed to make dry, brittle, sun-damaged hair, and hair that has been color treated or exposed to a lot of heat from a blow-dryer or a flat-iron (that's me – but don't judge), into soft, strong hair with improved manageability and shine. Another checkmark! (Oh, just a FYI, for those with sensitive scalps from what I've read, bananas have no known substances that can cause irritation.)

Armed with my research, the time came for the rubber to meet the road - for me to find out how well bananas would work on hair. Trying the bananas would be the true test. So, consider this me taking the hit for you.

First, I washed my hair as I normally would and left it damp. Then, I peeled and mash-up a banana in a bowl with a fork to make a sort of "banana paste." What happened next, wasn't supposed to happen, apparently I didn't read the fine print. You are supposed to mash the banana up *really, really, really well* ... like pudding *really well*, before putting it on the damp hair. Me? I only mashed it *really well* and spent the better part of an hour picking banana pieces out of my hair. So words to the wise ... mash the banana up *reeeeallllyy well*, or you too will lose a good hour of your life. Not Good.

Okay, back to my hair. After I removed all the banana chunks out of my hair, there was still a lot of the banana pudding conditioner left in the bowl, so I put it in my hair and worked it in. Next, I wrapped my hair up and put on a shower cap. You can also use a plastic grocery bag or saran wrap, but I chose the latter ... big mistake. I used my favorite shower cap, which became caked on the inside with slimy banana pudding conditioner and the elastic band smelled like ... yep, bananas. Word to the *even wiser*, you might want to get more shower caps and label them "banana conditioner only."

I left my hair up in the shower cap for about an hour, or so, and then rinsed the conditioner out. Oh, yeah and another thing, you might wanna have a bathtub strainer in the drain ... because even if thought you got all the banana chunks out ... you didn't, trust me.

There are tons of variations for using bananas to condition your hair on the internet so look away to see if you find one you like better. Like, for instance, peel two bananas and mash them up in a bowl using a fork until they are kinda lumpy. (Hey wait a minute! That's what I did!) But then, you mix a half a cup of honey in with the bananas and beat with a whisk or mixer. Geese details! Pour the mixture into a clean used shampoo bottle. And, then to use, just pour a small amount out and apply it to your clean hair, leave on for a few minutes and then rinse. Or, consider this recipe. Peel a banana and add a quarter cup of olive oil and one egg white to it. Place everything in a blender and purée it for a couple of minutes. Then, apply it to your damp hair – again leave on for a little while and rinse.

For me, trying to steer clear of all-things-electronic and seeking alternatives to store-bought grooming-aids, the lone banana mixture is still my choice of a deep hair conditioner. And, I have to say, even with all the comedy of errors – my hair turned out *soooo* soft and shiny! It looked fantastic when it dried!

As a recommendation, it is suggested you use the banana conditioner to treat your hair once a month, or for extremely dry hair, twice a month. You can bet I'm going to do it at least once a month as long as I can get my hands on bananas!

Now happily that bunch of bananas that usually just sit in the bowl on my counter begging for attention will now have a special purpose! Chalk one up for survival hair conditioner!

What You Can Do To Prepare

Seeking alternative to your preparedness items is a wise thing to do. As they say having back-ups to your back-ups. But what is just as important as these backups, is practicing with them. You don't ever want to find yourself in a situation where you aren't sure what the outcome will be to a backup plan – like my banana conditioner experiment that almost drove me bananas picking out the chunks! – Just sayin'.

Notes:

Oil Pulling:
A Must for Your Survival Plan

I am always on a quest to replace, substitute, or find alternatives to my preparedness and survival items, albeit a tool, self-defense method or food item. And, the same holds true for health and medicinal items as well. As the old adage goes, "an ounce of prevention is worth a pound of cure" and I have found this to be true in so many ways when using things we have growing in and around our homestead. Take honey for instance, a little dab of honey on a cut and it heals right up; avoiding infection. Have a sore throat? Take some elderberry syrup or a tablespoon full of elderberry jam, and nip those sniffles in the bud before they turn into a full-blown cold.

What I've learned by living pretty close to off the-grid is that it forces you to "make do" with what you have on-hand, something we all should strive for and try to practice a little more. For me, it has been a strengthener for sure.

I'm not a greenie or nature-ish type of person (no disrespect or offense intended to those of you who are), but I do know that when the poo hits the fan and all of our commercial items are used up, we will have to rely on the things we have growing in our gardens, like herbs and spices, and items in our food stores and pantries as major sources for anything and everything that ails us. Which, leads to the point in all this, I was chewing a piece of soft buttery garlic crust from my homemade Friday-night pizza one … well Friday night, when I felt this oddness on one of my back molars. I spit the bite of crust out in my hand (*ewwww!* I know) and raced to the bathroom mirror to look. Yep, I had broken a porcelain crown – a piece of it at least, the front part, the part most exposed for the entire world to see, with the back part securely in place almost tauntingly. Panicked, I dug through the partially eating bite of pizza, in hopes of retrieving the missing piece of crown (I know, gross, but go with me here – I was desperate!) Denied. I had eaten it. And, no, I did not consider waiting for the alternative ... so don't even go there (no pun intended.)

My first thought was ... it's Friday night and I have two long days before I could even hope to see the light of a dentist's office ... that is, if I could even get an appointment for Monday.

My mind began to race. "What would I do if this had happened after the poo had hit the fan?" A time where there would be no dentist office to go to. (I do a lot of this type of thinking by the way, the "what-if.")

Immediately I jumped on my computer (another thing we won't have when the poo hits the fan) to search the internet for something I could do in the interim to prevent any bacteria build up in the tooth ... and secretly hoping for some sort of miracle tooth regrowth cure. (One could hope.)

While in my search; as also happens ... a lot, I got a little sidetracked from my initial query of finding something to keep my "tooth" free of bacteria until I could get to a dentist, and stumbled upon ... oil pulling. I know this is going to sound kinda oxymoron-ish. How can you pull oil, right? But, intrigue set in and I began to research it further.

Oil pulling is nothing new, *really* nothing new; in fact it is an old Ayurvedic (or Ayurveda) medicinal practice that evolved in India thousands of years ago. This intrigued me

150

even more. If the people were using Ayurvedic medicine way back when, and still are today, it must be natural and healthy.

As most of us may know, just about all medicines on the market today originally began as natural ingredients. But the pharmaceutical companies began adding colors, chemicals, and additives to them, so who knows how much of the original ingredients are still in them today?

So back to oil pulling (caveat: this is going to sound really weird. I mean *really, really* weird.) The premise of oil pulling is this; by taking a tablespoon of vegetable based oil; such as sunflower oil, sesame seed oil, safflower oil, coconut oil, et cetera, and swishing it in your mouth for about 20 minutes, the oil acts as a detoxifier. As you work the oil around your teeth and gums while swishing, it "pulls" out bacteria and other debris from your body. The reason for the 20 minutes is it takes this long to break down the plaque and bacteria, but is not long enough for the body to reabsorb the toxins and bacteria. See? I told you it sounds weird.

Now, I know you are probably thinking, 20 minutes! I did too. But if you "pull" while taking a shower, fixing breakfast, or checking your emails, I promise the time is over before you even notice. How do I know? I tried it the very next morning using coconut oil. (NOTE: If the coconut oil is in a solid form at first, hold it under your tongue and it will melt.) The results were surprising! My teeth, which I am a little obsessive about anyhow, felt really clean. Like dental visit cleaning, clean.

While you are "pulling" the oil will become thicker. When you finally spit it out - NOT in the sink or toilet by the way ... we are talking oil here, it will become kinda white and foamy – if not you didn't swish long enough. I then rinse my mouth out with warm salt water and brushed my teeth as usual with baking soda and peroxide.

I have found that mornings are better for me to "oil pull" in fact, to get the most benefit; you are really supposed to do it on an empty stomach so you can get all the yucky things that have built up in your body and mouth during the night. But some people "pull" at all different times of the day.

Do your own research; which I always urge you to do, you will find that oil-pulling is associated with all kinds of benefits for other health issues, after detoxing the body of toxins Here are just a few of oil-pulling benefits:

Migraine headache relief

Correcting hormone imbalances

Reducing inflammation of arthritis

May help with gastroenteritis

Aids in the reduction of eczema

May reduce symptoms of bronchitis

Helps support normal kidney function

May help reduce sinus congestion

Some people report improved vision

Helps reduce insomnia

Reduced hangover after alcohol consumption

Aids in reducing pain

Reduces the symptoms of allergies

Helps detoxify the body of harmful metals and organisms

Fortunately, I'm pretty healthy and can't report on having any superpowers since my first oil-pulling experience, but I will tell you my skin is softer, my hair, eyebrows and eyelashes are thicker and I have the pinkest tongue *grin*. And why is having a pink tongue a big deal? Well, have you noticed how your doctor asks you to stick out your tongue during your check up? It's because the tongue can actually reflect diseases of the body and can show a lot about your overall state of health. Cool huh?

What You Can Do To Prepare

So why am I even talking about oil-pulling? Because our mouths are the gateway to all kinds of bacteria and toxins; including candida that causes gum disease and tooth decay, and can attribute to so many other health problems. It only makes sense that we would want to rid bacteria from the same place it enters.

Oil-pulling could be a very inexpensive and beneficial way to keep our teeth and gums healthy now and, if and when the poo-hits-the-fan. Think about it, we may no longer have access to store-bought toothpaste and oral hygiene products, but by using just one tablespoon of vegetable-based oil, some baking soda and 3% hydrogen peroxide we could keep our mouth germ free and our bodies healthier by ridding them of all those nasty toxins.

Oh, just a FYI. When I finally got in to see a dentist; after he examined my mouth, he commented on how clean and healthy my teeth, gums and tongue were. (I didn't tell him my little secret.) - Just sayin'.

Notes:

❧ 6 ❧
Fitness

Emergency Go Bag Challenge!

While speaking at Preparedness Conferences around the country, I have seen firsthand how hungry people are for knowledge and preparedness items (a good thing). I have watched; in amusement sometimes, as people load-up with bags, boxes and armfuls of "all-things-preparedness" items to stuff into their newly acquired emergency go-bags without; at least it appeared this way, giving much thought to the real use of their go-bags (not a good thing).

"I live on a homestead I don't need a go-bag." I've heard some say. Hmm. Well, listen up – unless you *never* travel off your property and/or live in an impenetrable fortress, we all need an emergency go-bag, or even better, several emergency-go-bags - for ourselves and each member of our family in case of an emergency evacuation or event.

When purchasing a go-bag, we might want to consider these questions: Is the bag durable enough to hold up under harsh conditions like inclement weather? Or from constantly putting it down on different types of terrains? Will the bag standup to all the contents you put in it? (A lot of us have loaded our bags so full of "anything-and-everything" preparedness without giving the least bit of thought to the weight of the bag)? And, can you walk with the bag on (let alone picking it up). Also consider this, in a poo-hits-the-fan event we may not have a vehicle to throw a go bag into, and therefore may have to really walk while wearing the bag.

Other concerns to consider with a go-bag are weight distribution and balance. Most of us find pockets and sections in our bag and just start cramming anything that will fit into them. Uneven distribution can actually make the bag more difficult for us to carry; resulting in physical strain and fatigue or worse, damage to the bag itself. If we are on foot and our bag is damaged, we could be in a heap of trouble. Have you ever tried to carry a ripped grocery bag full of groceries? Your one hand-carrying activity soon turns into a both hands and arms carrying activity. That's the type of "heap of trouble" I'm taking about.

We need to start thinking "smart packing" – not, hey here's another space I can shove something into. Because where you place items in your bag is just as important as the bag itself. Have some organization to your bag. I actually have a small guide that I had laminated that shows where things are in my bag – you might want to consider this too. It makes it so easy to know right where to go for something.

Now to the subject of weight, no, not yours, but we will get to that in a minute. Carrying 30 pounds versus 20 pounds is vastly different, especially over different terrain. Plus – as the saying goes "you get what you pay for" – so a cheap bag (not to be confused with a good one on sale), is not necessarily going to stand up to a lot of abuse.

We need to also physically start using our EDC, BOB, INCH, GHB, and Go-Bag (whatever your pet name is for your emergency bag.) How? Well, for starters, if nothing more, strap the bag on and walk around the house to "try it on for size." After all, we wouldn't buy a pair of shoes without trying them on and walking around the shoe department, would we? Do some simple chores while wearing the go-bag, then go outside and walk around. Doing these activities should instantly tell you if the bag has too many items in it, if it's unbalanced, and if you need to make some changes. Like for instance, foregoing some items, and using your skills and knowledge instead?

Make wearing your go-bag a challenge. If you have to adjust your bag weight do so but continue the challenge. Each time you put the bag on increase the distance you walk with it on. Walk on different terrains (grass, asphalt, gravel, snow, et cetera). Oh and when practicing to move fast wearing the bag, don't run instead jog, or shuffle. We don't want to beat up our joints with all that jostling.

If you find the bag is still unmanageable over a longer distance because you are winded, yet you can't live without the remaining in the bag, the next step would then be to increase your endurance. Remember when I said we would get back to your weight? Well here goes. Exercise, doing exercises like: air squats and thrusters (holding your bag in front of you, air squat, and then force the bag above your head while you stand), push-ups wearing your bag, crunches with the bag on your chest and pull-ups wearing the bag. These all simulate real-life movements – pushing, pulling, lifting, climbing, and will help increase muscular strength and endurance. (I know it wears me out reading these things too.) For some who are not used to exercising, these exercises may seem a little extreme - okay, a lot extreme. So maybe start with flexibility and dynamic stretching. Doing lunges while wearing the bag. Or try wall sits (backs to the wall), jump squats (not using the bag as this has potential to damage joints), flutter kicks (lying on your back and kicking your legs), or planks (a strength exercise that involves maintaining a difficult position for extended periods of time – like say in a push-up position with the body weight on forearms, elbows, and toes.)

What You Can Do To Prepare

Because I truly, believe being able to carry and maneuver with our go-bags is such an important prep skill – I would like to challenge you with a go-bag challenge. Pick-up your go-bags, get with your friends and/or family and create a group and start the challenge today (practicing in numbers will make us more accountable and encouraging of one another.) Remember start slow and work up in your endurance and distance. The first step is always the hardest. Keep in mind this challenge could mean the difference between life and death ... yours. – Just sayin'.

Notes:

Throwing a Fit Over Fitness:
Getting Into Survival Shape

Just so you know ... that is, if you don't already know, it doesn't matter how much you cram into that go-bag of yours, or how many survival books, magazines or blogs you've read, or even how fit you think you are, you are not ready until you have physically headed out the door into the wild blue yonder, bringing with you your knowledge, skills and all those supplies strapped to your back – and hopefully you survive to tell about it.

Most of us have our go-bags packed and ready to grab. We have survival knowledge and skills. And, some of us even consider ourselves fairly physically fit. (And by *fit* I mean you fall into the "normal fit" criteria of eating right, getting enough sleep, exercising and taking your vitamins. But, *vvvvrrrrrpppp* ... stop the press! Think again. We are not as fit or prepared as we think we are. Okay, so, let me put it this way by asking these questions. Are you prepared for walking in a heat index of 100° degrees all day and into the night? Are you prepared to walk in wet socks and shoes while being eaten alive by black flies and blood sucking mosquitoes? Are you prepared (oh the shame of it all) to sweat (yes, contrary to popular belief, girls do sweat by the way). Are you prepared to trample through tall grass, muddy water up to your knees, all the while subtracting and donning clothes as you go? And ... are you prepared to not have your hot or iced cocoa-chocolate-mocha-latte' frou-frou coffee drinks every two hours? This is a lot to think about, huh?

Have you ever noticed how coaches, whether it is athletic, musical, or otherwise stress the need to practice,

practice, and then practice some more? Am I right? And guess what? There's a method to this madness they call "practice"! The mere definition of practice should tell us something, "… learn by repetition; systematic training by multiple repetitions …" Key word here? It is repetition. You are doing something over and over.

Human natures tells us that because we have read all those books and have a bag packed full of "all-things-preparedness" that we are set; that we are prepared. Well I'll be the bearer of bad news, if you are thinking just this; you unfortunately are only fooling yourself into a false sense of security.

What You Can Do To Prepare

When was the last time you walked anywhere? And no, I don't mean to the mailbox at the end of your driveway and back. That doesn't count (well not so much). What I mean is, if you are not taking the stairs at work, or wherever you can take stairs instead of riding an elevator, you need to start – today. If you jump in your car every time you have to go to the store located right around the corner from where you live, you need to start walking to the store instead. "But I will have to carry my groceries home!" you whine. Well, duh?? Yes, you will. I hate to throw this at you, but you're gonna be carrying far heavier things in your go-bag than a couple of shopping bags full of groceries if and when, the poo ever hits the fan! In fact, you might want to purposely do all of your grocery shopping by walking to and from, as a way to start building up your endurance. Sounds painful, huh? That is the point. Bugging out will be painful too - very painful. And, if you really want to step it up, if it is raining out, forget the umbrella.

Forget the raincoat. Get out there and get wet. Really wet, like sopping wet. Yes, hair and all. Experience what it is like being cold and wet.

The bottom line here is that if there is a hard way to do something. Start doing it now. Try doing a lot of what you would normally do in the course of the day – the hard way. Stop taking the path of least resistance or the easy way. Life as we know it when the poo hits the fan will be hard; bordering at times on the impossible. The more we can do now to prepare the easier it might be in the long run. Oh, and speaking of "run" start practicing your running too. – Just sayin'.

Notes:

The "Stair" Master

So I'm thinking (scary I know), we really have no idea what is going to happen in a poo-hits-the-fan scenario, right? Think about it. If there is traffic congestion due to an unforeseen disaster, we may have just enough time to grab our emergency go-bag from our home or car, and start hoofing it. And, that is where my thought is going here ... the hoofing it part. So many of us, from age twenties and up, are feeling the effects of, eating all those happy-burgers, our sedentary lifestyle of watching on-demand movies, texting, working, and ... just plain ol' ... "I'm too tired to do anything".

Most of us spend two-thirds of our lifetime at work, and the other one-third eating, sleeping, going to the bathroom/grooming, watching TV and socializing. We are just not getting any exercise, are we?

If you have ever personally experienced a disastrous event, or at least seen one on television, then you know that there will be a lot of smashed, broken, mangled, and twisted things on the ground afterwards. Everywhere you look, in all directions, most likely you will see scattered debris. What this could mean to us, if we were caught up in a disaster, we may find ourselves cleaning all this stuff on the ground up or walking, climbing, or crawling around and over some of it, to get to a safe place. How in the heck do we even condition ourselves for what we may have to do after a disaster? I mean, of course, less us going to a playground and crawling around on the jungle-gym to get a "feel" for what it would be like crawling over, under and around things (which we might want to reconsider if we are thinking about it, because with all the wackos out there, moms could get pretty nervous seeing grown-ups playing on the playground equipment). But, then it dawned on me. Why not use stairs? You know those wooden or cement risers and treads that go up into the unknowns, and then back down into the abyss? Those things that are usually placed next to elevators and escalators, with banisters attached to them? No? Hmm. Okay this is gonna take more work than I thought.

Let's talk about some of the benefits to our bodies of using stairs. Think about the body and what parts we use when climbing stairs (less of course legs, heart, and lungs, which we know we will immediately feel). How about our arms we will cling to the handrail with and drag ourselves up? Or our buttocks, (caboose, behinny, rear-end, gluts, call it what you will, it's still gonna hurt) used to propel our legs to the next step? And, our stomach muscles to hold back that sick feeling once we've made it to the top of the stairs? Trust me it will all be worth it.

We *need* to exercise. Taking stairs requires no special skill (well we need to find them first), and just like walking, all we need to do is just put one foot in front of the other – just remember to lift the foot first. (Okay, so there *is* some special skill.) Just focus on taking one step at a time, and gradually work your way up to more steps or flights. (Like we would even make it up the first flight the first time around, right?)

And if you are a runner, here is something you might wanna know, just because you run does not mean you are a stair climber too. We all have this little thing called "gravity" working against us when climbing stairs. It's like having a ball and chain wrapped around your waist or you are physically carrying yourself up the steps. Also, stairs are steeper than most hills, so stairs many be a great alternative workout for you. (Ever see your runner pals run stadium stairs?)

So, why would we want to climb stairs anyhow? Uh, because we want to live – and survive - after the poo hits the fan? "But can't we use one of those stair thingies at the gym?" you ask. And the answer is, sure, but you won't get the same workout. Those stair *thingies* only work your legs. You will have awesome looking legs but you will still be out of breath taking the stairs - like runners (not hate'n.)

What You Can Do To Prepare

After an emergency disaster we are going to have to carry things while trying to maneuver around obstacles at the same time. We may have to bend down or crouch to conceal ourselves, and then spring back up to get moving again. For our safety, we need to get as physically conditioned, as possible to move up and down with little effort. Using stairs enables us to get in far better shape to walk and carry things, by helping us learn to carry our weight, and our go-bag on our backs (which could weigh about 20-30 pounds.)

I say, forget about all those high-priced workout machines and equipment and start using the stairs. Oh and when you get really good climbing stairs, try running up them. – Just sayin'.

Notes:

❧ 7 ❧

Medical-First-Aid

Where Is Thumbkin … Where Is Thumbkin: When Things Happen Unexpectantly

This is a little painful to write, both physically and mentally, but I write it as a reminder as to just how fast something can happen.

I was in the kitchen putzing around one day when my eye caught the crate of sweet potatoes that had been sitting for a few days now patiently waiting to be sliced and dehydrated. Resigned, I pulled out my brand new mandolin slicer - new as in it had never before been used. Sure, I had a fancy-schmancy mandolin slicer, and one that sat over top of a bowl, but this new mandolin was one you held with one hand and sliced down with the other hand – with no stand (that should have been my first clue.) I figured the new mandolin slicer would be easier to use than the others. (Funny, in a weird sort of way, how you get in your mind that if you've used an item they must all work the same. Not so.)

I washed the new mandolin careful not to cut myself on the sharp slicing blade. Then I set it aside while I cleaned the sweet potatoes, boiled some water, and prepared a bowl of ice. Holding the mandolin with my left hand I took a sweet potato and began slicing. Now, I didn't use the finger guard (*cringe*) because the potato I was slicing was every bit of eight inches long and my fingers were far enough away from the blade; or so I thought. I was about three slices in when it happened … that awful gut realization that you have just cut yourself. My thumb was bleeding profusely. The mandolin dropped from my hand as I immediately turned to the kitchen sink to put my thumb under cold water to stop the cut from bleeding; but the bleeding wouldn't stop.

So, with my left hand, I wrapped my fingers around my right thumb and held it tightly as I raised both hands above my head - (I'm kinda a pro at this, I am always getting a nick here or there with kitchen knives.) Still, the bleeding continued. I knew from past experiences that sometimes it takes a while for the clotting process to kick-in so I didn't panic, I just continued to walk around with my two hands in the air above my head, until I noticed the blood flowing down my arm. "Uh oh, not good" I thought. Now I'm not really sure why, but I didn't actually look at the cut when I put it under the faucet. Maybe I was thinking it was like one of those razor cuts you get on your leg while shaving ... you know the type it bleeds like a leaking sieve, but the cut itself isn't so bad.

I continued to walk around; both arms raised in the air, still waiting for the cut to clot, when I glanced over to the kitchen counter where I was working. There sitting on the counter, as pretty as could be was the side of my thumb; literally, from above the knuckle to the top of the thumb; across the nail bed; a perfect quarter-inch slice. "Uh oh, this is *really* not good."

Due to my history with kitchen utensils, I always give myself a little buffer before calling in the cavalry, i.e. my husband. I can usually doctor myself up before anyone (my hubby) notices, and therefore is none the wiser – less the bandages here and there. Only this wasn't one of those times. Sighing, I meekly called out to my husband on the radio, which we both wore (in case of such an emergency), knowing in a flash he would be standing in front of me, out of breath, asking what happened. Except that didn't happen, well the "*what happened*" part at least. As I sat on the stairs, blood continued to trickle down my arm, I pointed back to the kitchen and the "thumb piece" on the counter.

Instead of the usual; were you using this or wearing that questions, my husband grabbed the "pieces-part" of my thumb, put it in a baggie with some ice, called the emergency room to tell them we were heading their way – half-thumbed, as we jumped in the car to drive to the hospital some 35 minutes away.

When we arrived at the emergency room, I was treated more like a novelty than a patient. It seems half the hospital staff (it was a pretty small hospital) had never seen a mandolin slicer injury and were eager to come by and visit – not me – my partial thumb. I could overhear a lot of indistinguishable chatter outside the door of the examination room, as the parade of scrub-uniform clad hospital personnel paraded in and out of the room with comments such as "Wow that's down to the bone," or 'I didn't realize those things could cut that deep." "*Come on really???*" I thought. I felt like a human petri dish being examined under a microscope.

Getting just a little frustrated by all the traffic and the lack of treatment thus far – after all, I had been there an hour already, I asked the staff if they were "guessing" as to how to proceed. Almost, instantly the flow of "visitors" slowed and the staff began to focus on the injury.

When it was all said and done, my beloved thumb piece was not reattached, (something they said they no longer do - *sigh*). The staff applied a mesh dressing to the thumb divot, and then wrapped the thumb with gauze to five times its normal size. I was then sent on my way with two prescriptions; one for pain, and one for an antibiotic, and instructed to return the following day for "a wound check-up".

I returned to the hospital the next day; as instructed, which turned out to be an even worse visit than the first. After answering the same questions I answered not more than 24 hours earlier, I was then taken to an examining room to have my thumb looked at. For some unknown reason - at the time that is, the dressing was not coming off easily. First, the nurse had me hold the dressing under warm water for a while. Nothing. Then, I soaked it in warm water and peroxide. Still nothing. The nurse, a little perturbed at the time it was taking for the dressing to be remove, in frustration told me that I would just have to "bite the bullet" and pull it off. Thankfully, the doctor walked-in at that very moment and intervened. What the nurse didn't realize – gotta love the medical field - and the doctor explained to me later, was that the mesh had adhered deep into the wound. My thumb and the mesh were now one with one another. Had I "pulled" the dressing off, I would also have ripped out the little capillaries in the thumb as well. The long and short of it all, it took over two hours to remove the dressing. The ultimate remedy was a Novocain-type injection.

Needless to say, I did not return to the emergency room after that visit. For good or bad, I figured I could change my own bandages, and watch for infection just as well as they could. And, I did.

The thumb healed amazingly well treated with a daily application of pure raw honey and nothing more. And, today, the only residual of the initial injury, is a faint scar and a slight angle to the side of my thumb. No nasty indentations or numbness.

What You Can Do To Prepare

So why did I even share this? Because if this had happened to me; or you, during in a disaster scenario where there was no medical help available, this is a lesson for us all. And no, it is not – don't use sharp knives. The lesson is to not take shortcuts. I was so focused on the easiness of the mandolin that I didn't notice that it did not come with a stand. But I did notice there was no stand before I started to use it, and I still tried to use it anyway. And, to make matters worse, I didn't use the finger guard which is a huge no-no. (Okay you can judge – it was just plain stupidity on my part.)

Thankfully, some good came out of this "not so good" accident. I learned how incredibly awesome raw honey is for its healing properties and how invaluable it will be if, and when, the poo ever hits the fan, as part of our first-aid medical supplies. I firmly believe that if I would have continued going back for follow-up appointments on my thumb (however I am not suggesting you do this) that my thumb would not have had the same outcome as it did with the honey remedy. And another good thing, if the honey drips while you are applying it to your wound, you can just lick it up – you can't do that with medicine! (I'm just kidding!) - Just sayin'.

Notes:

Potassium Deficiency:
The Run on Potassium Iodide Tablets

In classic American "mass-hysteria" style, there was an increased demand for potassium iodide tablets in the United States after the devastating earthquake and the subsequent tsunami that struck Japan in 2011 and resulted in the nuclear meltdowns, and the release of radioactive materials at the Fukushima Daiichi Nuclear Power Plant.

Potassium iodide, which is not to the same thing by the way as the potassium that you find in bananas and other foods, or the supplement taken for conditions such as high blood pressure or heart disease, is a tablet (pill, capsule, or liquid) that you take to reduce the risk of thyroid cancer from exposure to iodine-131 (radioactive fallout).

To get a little medically here, potassium iodide should be taken; in a perfect world, two hours before any exposure to radioactive fallout, and up to four hours after. The potassium iodide saturates the thyroid gland with healthy iodine to block radioactive iodine from accumulating in the gland, thereby preventing radioactive Iodine-131 from entering the thyroid.

At the time of Japan's 2011 disaster, there were only three FDA approved companies in the United States who made potassium iodide; Anbex, Recipharm and Fleming Pharmaceuticals. We Americans were so edgy (and rightfully so) that we may experience exposure from radioactive fallout, that the stockpiles of potassium iodide were depleted - fast. Surprisingly, it wasn't just Joe and Jill American who were seeking potassium iodide. It was also the likes of pharmacies, hospitals, day-care-centers, and even places as far away as Singapore, Korea, and yes Japan. All were vying for this holy grail of a disaster pill.

After the 2011 disaster, "experts" (whoever they are) told Americans that the chances of dangerous amounts of radiation reaching the U.S. were small, and that there was absolutely no reason for concern or to take such precautions. Are you kidding me??? Holy lightning-bug Radioactive-Man! That is exactly what we need to do. Prepare ahead of time! Not wait and panic like the rest.

Each of us should already have a bottle of potassium iodide in our emergency kits or medicine cabinet, if not do so. Have you looked around at all the nuclear power plants we have here in our nation? They're like birthday candles on a cake waiting for lighting. Also, we are still experiencing nuclear radiation fallout from the meltdown of the reactors in Japan (you know the stuff we were told not to worry about?) Remember, once exposed, potassium iodide tablets will be of little use.

What You Can Do To Prepare

So, my point in all of this is to say, we can't wait for a catastrophic event here in the United States before we start to prepare. Be proactive and have your emergency kit assembled for any disaster; including nuclear radiation fallout.

There are 34 states that have residents living within 10 miles of a nuclear power plant. Of those 34 states, 22 states have potassium iodide tablets for every resident living within 10 miles of their nuclear power plant. Keep in mind there are 104 nuclear power plants here in the U.S. I'd rather take my tablet at home after hearing the first news of a radioactive disaster, then standing in line with a horde of panicked neighbors waiting for one, wouldn't you?

Now, there is a caveat for using potassium iodide; these tablets should only be used in the face of imminent threat of exposure to nuclear radiation. If taken inappropriately, they can do more harm than good. You know, like eating your dessert before you eat your dinner. (Yes you do.) – Just sayin'.

Notes:

That Burns My Hide:
Learning To Care For and Treat a Burn
In A Survival Situation

Okay, true confession time. Any type of heat source and I, always seem to go to battle every time we come in contact with one another. And, usually the heat source wins. I mean, it doesn't matter what the heat source is, it could be a hair straightener, the oven or the BBQ grill ... makes no difference, I walk away with a painful battle scar; a burn.

I'm sure we've all experienced a burn or two in our lifetime. Most, thank goodness, are generally surface wounds. But there are those burns that go much deeper. In fact, some burns are so severe that they penetrate down into the muscle or even the bone and blood vessels. Those are the serious burns.

So, let's say someone gets burned and we are living in a not so pleasant post-apocalyptic type world – with no medical help around. How do we treat that burn? Well first, we need to assess the burn. Look for blistering, sloughing of the skin or charred/blackened skin; these are signs that the burn has gone deeper than just a surface wound. As a visual guide; a first-degree burn will be reddish; a second-degree burn will have blistering; and, a third-degree has tearing of the skin. (Not being gross ... but pizza looking.)

For this example, say we are dealing with a first-degree burn. Next we need to stop the burning process. Soak the wound in cool water for about five minutes, or slowly pour water over it. Then, remove any dirt and debris on and around the burn by gently washing the area with soap and water. Apply aloe Vera gel or a topical antibiotic cream to the burn and cover it with a sterile non-stick-pad or dressing. For pain relief, and to reduce any swelling, you can give the person acetaminophen or ibuprofen. Luckily, a first-degree burn is a surface type wound and should heal fairly quickly. However, with all burn wounds you should watch for infection.

If the person has sustained a second-degree burn, this is a little more serious of a burn. Remove any clothing or jewelry near the burn area as these things can retain heat. Cool the burn area and clean it with soap and water (hopefully you have a first-aid kit to work out of, if not you need to get one or make one), make sure to gently remove any debris by splashing water on the burn or wiping the wound; be cautious to not break the blister, this is nature's way of protecting the wound and keeping out infection. Pat the burn dry and apply antiseptic ointment with a cotton swab or tongue depressor – really slathering the ointment on like cake icing – this will create a barrier to keep infection out. Then, apply a non-stick sterile pad over the burn area (again if you don't have these – you know the drill – get them.) To reduce swelling and minimize the pain, apply some type of cool compress to the injury on and off for ten minute intervals and give a pain-reliever such as ibuprofen or acetaminophen. If at all possible, re-dress the burn twice a day – you might have to soak the dressing first to remove it – then redress the wound.

Third-degree burns are the grosses and the worst possible burns a person can have; and the most life-threatening. In a normal world these burns would require admittance to a burn unit for treatment. For us in a post-poo-hits-the-fan world, the best we can do is monitor the person for responsiveness and breathing; cover the burn(s) lightly with sterile non-stick dressing; and if possible, elevate the burned area higher than the person's heart. If the person's face has a burn, sit them up; keep them warm and comfortable. Monitor for shock and treat accordingly. Needless to say, for a third-degree burn, the best thing you can do for the person injured is to find someone with profession medical training.

What You Can Do To Prepare

Please understand this information is in no way to give medical advice, it is merely for you to use as a guide in a dire situation where there are no doctors available (or around), and no medical help available. If you haven't done so, you might want to consider taking a first-aid course on how to treat all stages of burns.

Having an emergency kit with first-aid supplies readily available and accessible can minimize the chances of the burn injury worsening or developing an infection. If by some chance you don't have sterile dressing and gauze available in your first aid kit, you will have to make a covering out of a clean cloth to keep dirt out and avoid infection in and around the burn. Remember infection in burns is the enemy, so the wound has to stay clean.

Some suggested items to include in your emergency medical first-aid kits are: gauze, adhesive, wound dressings, antibiotic ointments and creams, antiseptics and disinfectants like peroxide, isopropyl alcohol, antiseptic wipes, aspirin, Tylenol or ibuprofen, medical tape, disposable gloves, and scissors. These suggestions are just the tip of the iceberg. Do your homework. Get the items suggested to assure you are prepared. The burn could be yours next time. – Just sayin'.

NOTES

A Sticky Situation:
Using Super Glue as Sutures
In A Survival Situation

Okay, I admit it; I would have a hard time physically watching someone injured being sewn-up by another person. Even on television, a movie, or a documentary watching the stitching process "creeps me out" big time so I usually watch through laced fingers over my face. There's just something about the skin being pulling up with that hooked needle that gives me the heebie jeebies. Now, don't get me wrong, if I had to, I'd sew somebody up in a heartbeat, but that's because my fight or flight responses would kick in, it would definitely not be because I was saying, *"Oooohhhhh, pick me, pick me!"*

So, why do we even sew-up ... okay stitch-up wounds in the first place? Most of the time, by bringing the two sides of the lacerated tissue together it creates pressure to help stop any bleeding. And stitching also helps prevent infection by closing up the wound. Our bodies heal from the inside out – so by bringing the wound together it helps keep the bad things out during the healing process.

Now the question is, are there alternatives to sewing? Okay, okay, stitching. Let's say you were injured; a pretty good size cut on your arm, and you were all by your lonesome, just you, and your lowly emergency medical first-aid kit to do the repairing? What could you use to repair that laceration?

For, starters as an alternative, there is skin tape (Steri-Strips); a thin adhesive strip that you use to close small wounds. They are easy enough to use, you just apply a strip to one side of the injury, and pull it across to the other side, making sure to line the sides up with one another as best you can.

Then, there is glue; also known as tissue adhesive. I did a little digging on this one and learned that Super Glue-type and medical cyanoacrylate glue; used in hospitals and doctors' offices, are apparently identical in composition. The really big difference is in the cost. $2 if purchased from a store and $200 at the hospital - yep sounds about right. I have seen Super Glue used lots and lots of times by my father who worked with sheet metal and always kept a tube in his toolbox. It works really well. In fact, I have also used Super Glue a couple of times on myself after a kitchen knife wound, or two. To use the glue, first clean the laceration really well using warm water and soap; irrigate it to remove any dirt, then dry it and place small beads (droplets) of the glue at the ends and a few spaced out along the laceration. There's no need to apply a heavy line of glue, it usually won't hold as well if you do. The glue will begin to sloth off around three to seven day – which is usually more than enough time for healing of the laceration. And, it doesn't scar as bad as sutures (sometimes not at all!)

Then there are staples. Hmm. There's something about a staple gun and shooting staples into someone's body that gives me the willies too. (Of course that could come from the time I stapled my finger to a stack of papers.) In all actuality they say skins staples are a great way to pull wounds together, it is fast, and not that expensive.

Now to the good ol' sutures, yes we are back to that "*eeeeek*" subject for me. It is advisable to have a suture kit in your first-aid kit, but unlike glue, tape and staples this method requires some skill, and both of your hands to perform it.

Initially, before you decide on a method to close a wound or if you even need to close it, you need to consider the type of laceration; the depth and length. Next, thoroughly clean the wound with an antiseptic antibacterial solution and cut away any dirty and/or dead skin from the laceration. Then, choose the method for closing it.

What You Can Do To Prepare

If you have the basic skills to sew on a piece of clothing, such as a loose hem or rip, you can most likely suture a wound. You just need to decide what size medical needle and thread to use and what type stitch. Again, if you are going to consider this method (sutures), I would highly suggest you take some medical courses and/or do more research into different types of lacerations; what size sutures to use; and, how to treat wounds on or near joint areas.

As for Me, I'm sticking with Super Glue as my "go-to" – it's easy, you can apply it with one hand, it doesn't take up a lot of space, and it's inexpensive. In fact, I keep several tubes around the house and in my first-aid kit – just in case.

Oh, darn it! I just glued my fingers together again. - Just sayin'.

Notes:

Life-Saving Chest Workout:
Continuous Chest Compressions (CPR)

When most of us hear "CPR" we instantly think putting our mouth over and/or near someone else's mouth, and well ... that's just not okay with a lot of us ..., okay most of us. It is one thing to perform CPR on a dummy while in a training class where the mood is a little lighter and upbeat. It's another in its entirety to perform CPR in a real life emergency on someone who is bleeding from an injury, or has vomitus or foaming coming out their mouth, or even chewed up food still in their mouth, right??? (*Ewwww!*) In fact, I would venture to say that a lot of us would rather stand around in hopes that someone else steps up to the plate so we don't have to in an emergency such as this. Shameful, I know. But it's true. And, besides, who the heck can remember the ratio between chest compressions to-breaths?

Well there's good news! Good news and CPR? Yep, there's a new form of CPR developed by the doctors at Mayo Clinic. The doctors say there is enough oxygen in the blood to keep the brain supplied for ten minutes. Performing chest compressions would keep the blood flowing to the brain, heart and other organs – which is the whole reason we perform CPR in the first place.

So, in light of these new developments, *The America Heart Association* has also changed the CPR guidelines too - to chest compressions only, dropping the mouth-to-mouth part. What does this mean to us? No more breathing in someone else's mouth. Yay!!!!

The new procedure requires that you apply rapid (about 100 compressions per minute) and, deep presses to the center of the chest by placing your palm right in line with the nipples of the victim.

Now, I have heard people say they are afraid they might hurt the person by pressing too hard. Here's a FYI, if the victim has suffered cardiac arrest they are near death already and you can't hurt an "almost" dead person, right? I mean, what person wouldn't trade a couple broken ribs for life? So press hard moving as quickly as you can. It will be tiring, but don't stop until medical help arrives. And yes, if you are doing it right you are more likely than not going to break some ribs.

Oh and here's another useful tip. You can perform the hands-on chest compressions CPR to songs to help you keep the rhythm. In a trial study of medical students performing CPR to the song *Stayin Alive* by the Bee Gees, they maintained close to the ideal rhythm of 100 compressions per minutes (the song has 103 beats per minute). Not a big disco fan or even know what disco is? There are other songs you can use too, like *Another Bites the Dust* by Queen, *Cecila* by Simon and Garfunkel, *Hard Handle* by The Black Crowes, *Sweet Home Alabama* by Lynyrd Skynyrd, *Rock Your Body*, by Justin Timberlake, *I Will Survive* by Gloria Gaynor, *MMMBOP* by Hanson, *Girls Just Wanna Have Fun* by Cyndi Lauper, *Gives You Hell* by The All American Rejects and *Heartbreaker* by Mariah Carey. Something for everyone!

Whatever song you choose, remember to focus on the 100 compressions per minute. Oh and maybe, depending on what song you choose, you might want to sing the song not necessarily out loud, but to yourself.

What You Can Do To Prepare

Here's a little refresher on how to perform chest compressions (CPR). Place the heel of one of your hands in the center of the victim's chest (in between the nipples), then place the heel of your other hand on top of the first hand, and lock your fingers. Then, with your elbows locked begin forceful chest compressions. You will have to get over the "I'm hurting this person" and put your focus and energy more on applying hard compressions and trying to save someone.

Remember 100 compressions. Now everyone altogether ... *"Whether you're a brother or whether you're a mother, You're stayin' alive, stayin' alive. Feel the city breakin' and everybody shakin', And we're stayin' alive, stayin' alive. Ah, ha, ha, ha, stayin alive, stayin alive. Ah, ha, ha, ha, stayin alive* ... – Just sayin'.

Notes:

❧ 8 ❧
Food

Do You Really Know What You Are Paying For? Prepping On A Budget

One day I decided I would try to start eliminating the need to go to the grocery store so often; you know the teat of the consumer-mindset? As most may know, I began my journey into a more self-reliant lifestyle when I jumped off the corporate bandwagon (leaving a six figure income and cashing in my 401k) and headed for the "hills" ... sans the heels (*whaaaa*!! I miss my shoes!!!) I was the poster child for the consumer-minded.

I started my elimination process, by going through my past grocery store receipts to see where I was actually spending the most on "consumer products." You know, those items we use and discarded, only to replace them with more? That's where the consumer part comes in; we consume regularly and discard a lot.

The first question I asked myself was how often did I go to the grocery store? The second question was how can I go out to the barn to feed the animals and still wear high heels? (I'm just kidding! I digress.) It was, how often do other people go to the grocery store? After a little research, I learned that for some people, it is a lot. Like, once a week for actual groceries, and one to three times thereafter for milk and those "oops I forgot _____ (fill in the blank)" items, and that didn't include big box store shopping which was a whole other shopping trip entirely.

So, how can we work towards not going to the grocery store so often? Well, this is how I did it. I started with a list as any good preparedness-minded person would do. Not a shopping list, but a running list of things we were getting low on. I could see what "consumer products" were being used the most and our trend on using them.

Then I started thinking of some alternatives for these items – after all I was now living a more "self-reliant lifestyle." So let's take paper towels for instance. These were a recurring item on my list. I was using paper towels left and right – all day long. I hate wet hands so I would grab a paper towel any time my hands were wet. If something spilled on the counter, I'd wipe it up with a paper towel. If something dropped on the floor … well you get the idea, I was using a lot of paper towels. I began to consider what I could use instead. Like a dishcloth for clean-ups and spills. Or a dish towel to dry my wet hands off. I usually let my dishes air dry after hand washing so there was no chance of getting icky germs on my dishes from me drying my hands on a dish towel.

Next was toilet paper. Don't worry, I'm not going to suggest you use the pages out of your phonebook – although you might want to consider it if the poo-hits-the-fan as an alternative! What I will suggest, is making your own family *Hiney Hydrant* ™ - a portable survival bidet made from a simple inexpensive garden sprayer (go to my website to see how to make one.) And paper napkins? I now use colored wash clothes that match my dining room décor and are strictly dedicated to the dinner table. I was able to eliminated, paper towels, toilet paper, and napkins with alternatives.

Now let's talk spending. If you have $100 budget for groceries, make it count. I started taking a calculator with me to the grocery store – I know it's a pain, but it works! It's amazing how this method helps with those "should I get this or not" decisions when you tally items as you go. It is amazing at how true to your budget you will stay, and save by inputting the price of a product as you go. Oh, and keep in mind while you shop that "convenience" will cost you a lot more.

Begin to look at the unit cost of products rather than the retail cost. The unit cost, is what the item cost per pound, per ounce; per gallon; well you get the idea. This information is usually on the shelf label next to the price. Compare the unit cost with products of like units around it, including on the shelves above and below that item. And, while we are speaking of comparative brands, this leads me to something a lot of us fall into ... the store brand (private label) versus the national "spend-a-lot-of-money-on-the-wrapper-label-and-advertising" type products. Yes, the labels are prettier, brighter, and more happy-happy joy-joy on the name brands. But you are paying for that "papered-joy" in the way of the cost of research and development, packaging, advertising, and marketing. If you haven't already done this before, just for grins and giggles; and to save you a lot of money later, compare the unit prices of a store brand versus national brand. Let me share a little secret with you, some of the same companies manufacture both the store brands (private labeled) and the national brands so you are actually getting the same product in each. And, just so you won't feel like you are the only one buying the "cheap-chips" (my term of endearment for the store brand products), almost two-thirds of shoppers say that their grocery carts are usually filled with at least half store-brand products.

What You Can Do To Prepare

When it all comes down to it, food is food. I doubt very much that when hard times come around; and they will, that you or anyone will turn their noses up to a can of food because it is a store brand, right? Shopping store brands can actually save you on average 30 percent. So, remember our budget of $100? Those savings add up to more than $1,500 a year. That is $1,500 to spend on preparedness supplies! So get out your store receipts and start that list!

You might even save enough to get that awesome pair of … nah, again I digress. – Just sayin'.

NOTES

Food Insurance:
You Can Never Have Enough Insurance

I was preparing a box of macaroni and cheese for lunch one day (What??? Don't judge), and as I was stirring the noodles in the pot of boiling water I thought, "Noodles and powdered cheese, hmm. Hey, I'm making survival pantry food!" Dehydrated noodles and dehydrated cheese (Oh, yeah and the added junk they put in the mix to preserve it.) Well this got me to thinking about all the 'boxed' food I've prepared in a lifetime. (It's a lot by the way.) I wondered, could I copycat boxed foods to make my own survival pantry foods? I mean, think about it. By dehydrating food, either by using a dehydrator, an oven, or even the sun we could make a lot of those boxed meals that we loved as a kid (and some of us still do today), then using a vacuum sealer, some jars and bags, we could create away!

The search was on! Milk comes in a powdered form, butter comes in a powdered form, cheese comes in powdered form, and yep, even eggs come in a powdered form too. Then, there is the cooking and baking stuff; like sugar, flour, oats, grains, baking soda, baking powder, and powdered sugar. With these things added to our dehydrated fruits, veggies, meats and nuts, we could make just about anything and everything. Soups and stews; casseroles, rice dishes, pasta dishes, cake, cookie and muffin mixes, energy bars, you name it. We would be limited only by our own imagination!

And another thing, have you seen the prices on some of those MREs? (Military talk for 'meals ready to eat'), we would be better served to make our own meal packages. And by making them, we wouldn't have to worry about things like how long something has sat in a hot warehouse or the expiration dates – and the food we make would look a lot more pleasing too!

We can begin to make, or add to our survival food supplies, by using items we have in our pantry, cupboards and cabinets.

Nutrition is one of the keys to survival – well nutritional food that is. It's important that we don't eat a lot of empty calories. By the same token, food is also a comfort to us as well. Admit it, we get bored easily. So the more variety and selections we can have in our food choices, the better we will be able to adapt and survive during a catastrophic event.

Look at the list of things below that we should have in our survival pantries. Consider them an insurance policy against starvation. Make your own list of these items and do a checks and balance to see what you have and what you might need to get.

Baking powder
Baking soda
Bread crumbs
Broth (dried and canned)
Beans (all varieties; dried and canned
Coffee and tea (beans, ground, and instant)
Cocoa powder
Cornmeal
Cornstarch
Chocolate (unsweetened squares, semisweet and chips)
Cooking spray
Cereal (all kinds)
Crackers (different types)

Dried fruits: (raisins, apricots, pineapple, cranberries)
Extracts: (vanilla, lemon, almond, orange (heck get them all)
Flour (all kinds, i.e. wheat, rice etc.)
Garlic (dehydrated and fresh)
Granola (all kinds)
Jelly (jams, preserves)
Milk (boxed, powdered, evaporated milk
Meats (dried/dehydrated beef, tuna, chicken etc.)
Nuts (all kinds, i.e. peanuts, walnuts, almonds etc.)
Onions (dehydrated)
Pasta: (all kinds, i.e. spaghetti, linguini, angel hair, fettuccine, penne, noodles)
Peanut butter
Pepper
Potatoes (dehydrate all kinds)
Powdered eggs
Rice (all kinds; long, brown, regular, wild etc.)
Soups (all kinds)
Salt (or salt alternatives)
Spices/Oils (all kinds for both)
Sauces (canned for browning and flavor)
Sugar (granulated, confectioner's, light and dark brown)
Veggies (all kinds of dried/dehydrated)

What You Can Do To Prepare

Just as with home, automobile, life insurance, and your survival food storage, you can have just enough to get by with (just the basics) or you can have an umbrella policy which fills in the gaps and protects you over and above the basics.

Isn't insurance after all, in and of itself, a form of risk management to safeguard against the unknown? Am I right? So go make yourself some more insurance! – Just sayin'.

Notes:

Gift in a Jar:
Food That Can Really Go Far

Have you ever gotten one of those jars with a cocoa mix or a cookie mix in them from someone at the holidays or as a gift? I have many times. And, more often than not, the jar just sits on the counter for a while; mostly because it really looks cool with all the colorful sections; like sand art, and I don't want to destroy the pretty presentation ... I mean gotta love an artsy-craftsy person, right? But, in time, the jar goes up in the cabinet with all my other mixes.

But one year, I received something different in a jar. It was a gift of ... soup? The jar was still in the pretty little layers, but instead of a cookie mix, or a cocoa mix ... it was a soup mix. What?! No sweets or treats?! What's up with that I wondered? I wasn't sure about this soup jar gift. I had always considered the cocoa or cookie mixes as an "in case of emergency break open" sort of treat. Who wants soup, hmm? Hey, wait a minute! We do!

I began to analyze the soup jar to see what the heck was actually in it. The label said, "Chicken and Rice Soup." Okay, it had wild rice, dehydrated minced onion, vegetable flakes, chicken bouillon granules, thyme leaves, dehydrated minced garlic, dried marjoram, lemon pepper, and a bay leaf. Yummy! I was already getting hungry! A pattern began to emerge in my mind. Everything was dry! (Bear with me I'm a little slow at times.) The directions on the jar stated that all I had to do was add water and some chicken. "Just add water and chicken?" Eureka! This was survivor food! All in one beautiful presentation!! What a gift huh? Well the idea in the jar sure was! After all, I had canned chicken, and chicken in a can too, so if I added chicken to the soup mix in a jar and I had a meal!

I began to hunt for other "jar recipes" on the internet and found there are hundreds of them out there. We could have ready-made meals, by making these recipes, putting them in a food-saver-type bags, or mason type jars and sealing them for long-term storage. Why settle with just rice and beans for dinner when you can have a delicious hot steamy bowl of rice and chicken soup?

As I scoured all the many recipes out there I noticed that some called for adding meat to the dry ingredients. But that's no problem for us, like I said before we can add our canned meats, or meats we have canned. I have even dehydrated ground beef to make hamburger rocks. You can also use your homemade tomato sauce that you canned to the ingredients and there's your meal!

And listen up! You can also make mixes for drinks and snacks ... breakfast to dinner, and desserts too with these recipes. Doesn't get any better than that does it?

What You Can Do To Prepare

Whoever thought of these "gifts–in-a-jar" probably had no idea that they were actually creating a gift that was far greater than fresh cookies and hot cocoa!! Not only did they create meals that would make a quick meal for that person on the go, but they also created meals that you can store and use in time of an emergency too!

Picture this, you are with your prepper group practicing bug-out maneuvers (which by the way, you should do often), and while everyone is taking a break eating their peanut butter sandwich lunch, they longingly watch as you sit in front of your little sterno grill heating up water ... for that yummy meal of spaghetti and meat sauce. Now that is surviving! Now pull up a chair and let's eat! – Just sayin'.

Notes:

Gimme Some Sugar!
Honey the Other Sugar

One day, early on in my prepping journey, I had a friend come by for a morning visit. I was a little embarrassed when I realized I didn't have any sugar *after* offering her a cup of coffee. "Do you have any honey?' my friend asked after my comment of having no sugar. I thought to myself, "Honey instead of sugar in coffee?" It didn't sound too appetizing to me. Fortunately, for my guest, and me too, I did have honey. As my friend sipped her coffee, she told me that honey was actually better for us than sugar. I looked over at her, smiled in agreement (thinking all the while – yeah right – there's nothing better than sugar.) But, when my friend left, curiosity got the better of me and I tried a little honey in my coffee. And, ya know, I was pleasantly surprised.

While cleaning up after the visit with my friend, my mind went back to her comment about honey and being better for us than sugar. I wondered if it were true or just a personal preference. So, I decided to look into the pros and cons of both honey and sugar.

In my research, I found that both honey and sugar have glucose and fructose, which meant absolutely nothing to me. I wouldn't know one "ose" from the other. So, I continued on. Hmm, it appears that during the manufacturing process that heat destroys all the good stuff in sugar, but honey is only subjected to a minimal amount of heat during processing. Again … *whoop-dee-doo*, which one is gonna make my hiney bigger, is what I wanted to know. One tablespoon full of table sugar has about 46 calories. One tablespoon of honey has about 64 calories.

Ah, ha! That's it! Honey is better for you, but it also makes you fatter! Figures. Then, I read on. Oops, my bad. You actually use less honey because it is sweeter than sugar. Okay, so one for honey.

Next I learned that when we eat sugar our stomach has to use its own enzymes to separate the molecules apart before we can use the sugar's energy (all this chemistry-ish stuff, ugh!) With honey the bees have added a special enzyme to the nectar that divides the sucrose into glucose and fructose so our bodies can absorb directly. Well isn't that special. (I haven't a clue what this all means.) Oh wait, I just found out. It means that honey has slower absorption and infusion of sugars into our bloodstream for more of a gradual and healthier digestion process. Okay, two for honey.

Sugar lacks minerals and vitamins. In other words, it has empty calories. And sugar relies on our body's nutrients to metabolize it into our system, so, when these nutrients are all used up it obstructs our metabolizing cholesterol and fatty acid. And, that is what contributes to higher cholesterol and obesity! It's all due to higher fatty acid on the organs and tissues. And what that means to us? Yep, it can make us fat!

What You Can Do To Prepare

So it appears that honey is in fact the better choice for us health wise, then sugar. This is good news, especially for those of us who have beehives as part of our preparedness plan. (If you don't, you might want to consider adding a hive or two.)

Honey is nature's energy booster and it is a great immunity system builder. (Ever hear of someone taking a tablespoon of honey when they were feeling a little puny?) Honey is also a natural remedy for so many ailments. I have even used it for a topical remedy on cuts for its antibiotic properties. And, boy does honey make your skin soft! Apply a little on your face after a shower ... you'll see!

Caveat: raw/natural honey should never be given to infants under the age of two, due to botulism toxin, which infants are not able to break down and metabolize (this goes for immuno-compromised young children and adults as well). As adults, we are resistant to botulism toxin due to long-term exposure to the toxin in small quantities

Honey is man's oldest sweetener ... and now women's new best friend! – Just sayin'.

Notes:

WHAT COULD POSSIBLY GO WRONG???

Happy Burgers:
What is Really in Our Food?

"Step away from the happy burger counter!" said in my best and deepest, megaphone-type voice. Have you ever noticed how a lot of the happy burger-type restaurants (fast-food chains) are helping us in this tough economy by creating "not-a-lot-of-dough" menus? Or, as most refer to them as ... *The Dollar Menu* or *Value Menu*. And, speaking of Dollar Menus, isn't it funny how the dollar symbol ($) looks like we are paying less than when using the word "Dollar"?

We are programmed to think we are getting a good deal if we buy items from a dollar menu, right? Unfortunately, that couldn't be farther from the truth! Here is what happens. We walk up to the counter. We glance up at the menus and our eye catches sight of the dollar menu. We're amazed at how "cheap" everything is. So we order, after all everything is just a dollar! We order a happy burger, fries, a dessert, a fountain drink, and a shake. What we have managed to do is to spend more on our lunch then what we would have paid most times for a "value meal," the big brother to the dollar menu. But this is exactly what the restaurant was hoping you would do! Also, (now this may hurt) we have just managed to rack up a whopping 3,000+ calories for our lunch. That's right, all this simply by ordering off the Dollar Menu!!

Reality check from the bearer of bad news (me) ... to survive a disaster scenario, we need to start thinking nature's food – grown on land and in the sea. Like nuts, veggies, fruits, meats, fish, poultry, and dairy - caveman-style cuisine. "Ugh, me not like!!" said in my best caveman voice. I know I hear ya! "Where's the flavor in that stuff?" you ask. That "flavor" that you speak of and have become accustomed to, is nothing more than preservatives, and … grease. (*Sorry!*)

Currently there are over 3,000 food additives registered with the FDA. In the United States, there are nearly 10,000 new processed food products introduced each year; almost all of them include flavor additives. Sounds good huh? Not so yummy after all.

Think about this, happy burger restaurants will be a thing of the past should a disaster event strike. Well that is, unless you consider some entrepreneurial-ish guy setting-up his gas grill and bartering road kill meat burgers in exchange for supplies and gear?

What You Can Do To Prepare

It is time we start conditioning ourselves and bodies to eat from the earth instead of out of a bag. Start now before something not so good happens, to give our systems time to adapt. Our bodies need to adjust to new foods or food we are not used to eating often. Case in point, think of the time you ate something new at dinner and were reminded of what you ate later that night and possibly several times the following day too, as you sat in the bathroom. We won't have *that* luxury if we are trying to focus on protecting ourselves, family, and property (unless you tie a bucket to your hiney – but I don't see that working out too well.)

By eating caveman-style (food from the garden and food on the hoof), we are fueling our body with more protein and less fat, which in turn will make us stronger and healthier. And, when that not so good event happens, and we have to no other choice but to eat veggies, or sip hot homemade soup from a cup – it will actually taste good and we will know what we are eating and where it came from too!. – Just sayin'.

Notes:

Hard As a Rock Bread:
Making Hardtack Survival Bread

I was wondering how people would bake bread if they were "on the move" (as in bugging-out) and didn't have access to a loaf of bread or even a piece of bread for that matter. Well as with most things, this question got the best of me and I had to know what people did. The answer I found was a hard-type of bread known as "hardtack." Now, to me, and maybe you too, growing up as a kid, hardtack was that break your teeth surgery sweet holiday candy that came all stuck together in a brightly colored Christmas metal tin. The hardtack I'm talking about here is a break your teeth floury biscuit ... of sorts (*of sorts* literally).

It seems the concept of flour hardtack dates way back. It was used on long sea voyages by the military, explorers, prospectors, and pioneers. Now the name has changed down through the years from hardtack to such names as; ship biscuits, sea biscuits, cabin bread, sea bread, dog biscuits, tooth-dullers, sheet iron, worm castles, molar breakers (see where my "break your teeth" comment comes from?)

"So, what exactly is hardtack?" you ask. Well, it's more of a cracker than bread – a *reeeealllly* hard, bland cracker. And, from what I have read no wonder we slather anything and everything on our crackers today – this custom must have originated from hardtack eaters.

I have to say after investigating this little morsel, of fossilized stone, it sounds like it was more for "having something in your stomach" then it was for any nutritional value. Way back when, most medical issues dealt with digestion problems, so having "something" in your stomach could help avoid illness. Hmm.

Hardtack was ideal because it was portable, light weight and had a long shelf life. Case in point, after the Civil War, hardtack was stored, and then the surplus was used during the Spanish American war 35 years later! *Yumm-eeee!*

The surprising thing about hardtack is that it is still made today. In fact, Alaskans still eat it as part of their normal diet with melted butter, soup or moose stew (for us I guess that would be deer or rabbit stew).

What You Can Do To Prepare

We should always look for alternatives in all our preps. In my quest to find alternative bread, I found hardtack. I have to say for all the bad, hardtack does have some nutritional benefits, so this is why I am sharing this. I made some. And, they are right, it was bland, but I knew it would be. I just smeared some jam and butter on it and dunked it in my coffee. And yes, it would do in a pinch.

Now, if you are feeling a little adventuresome too, I have included the recipe. It's pretty simple, flour, water and a little salt. That is the novelty of this cracker. And, if kept dry, you can take it wherever you go because it is light-weight and endures extreme temperatures. Here's the recipe. Six parts flour to one part water. Do not put any shortening or oil on your hands. Knead dough until thoroughly mixed. Roll it out on a floured surface until it is about 1/8 inch thick (or there about). Cut into squares or rectangles depending on your preference (say the size of a Saltine or graham cracker example: 3 x 4 inches). Make little holes in the hardtack like crackers are today using the tines of a fork (make sure the holes go all the way through the dough). Bake the hardtack at 325 degrees for at least an hour, turning it over once. When done, the hardtack will still look pale. Let it cool overnight (so it gets that hard and dry feeling.) Note: Some people bake their hardtack at 300 for a couple of hours, just to get it really dry.

Remember hardtack got its name honestly. This stuff is hard. To eat hardtack, you will need to dunk it in your beverage of choice, or top it with some jelly, and peanut butter, and more butter, and some bananas slices, and some honey, and a few marshmallows, and cake sprinkles, and some pineapple slices, and cinnamon, and ... well any other toppings you can think of!!! "Polly-wanna-cracker?" – Just sayin'.

Notes:

Popcorn:
The Survival Comfort Food

Have you ever caught the smell of a co-worker's afternoon snack of microwave popcorn wafting through the halls and through the air vents? Or, as you enter the movie theater you are instantly hit with that wall of fresh popcorn popping? Our comments are usually always the same, "*Ummmm ...* that smells *sooooo* good!"

There is just something about hot buttery popcorn (okay, genuine artificially flavored butter syrup) that everyone loves, isn't there? And, popcorn is about the easiest and healthiest snack you can make. Not to mention, this is the snack that gives you the most bang for your buck.

I was thinking, what a great item popcorn is to include in our emergency food supplies. After all, we eat over one billion pounds of popcorn per year here in the United States, half of which, I'm sure was consumed by me! Now, I know what you're going to ask because I did too. How are we going to make popcorn without a microwave in a survival situation?

Popcorn is nothing new. Just because we can now buy it by the caseload in those little individually wrapped cellophane envelopes of buttery goodness, believe it or not, people made popcorn or popped corn – since the beginning of time (kinda), and without a microwave.

In the past; a long time ago, people popped corn using all types of creative methods. From using hot stones, to pottery with heated sand and even mesh wire baskets.

And why do corn kernels even pop? Well without getting to science-y, from what I understand, inside the thick hull of the corn kernel is a bunch of proteins and starches, oh, and some water. As the kernels heat up, the moisture inside turns to steam and eventually ... like with a lot of things that steam – "thar she blows!!" The hulls burst and the liquefied starch explodes then rapidly cools and hardens. And, that is how we get popped corn. Cool huh?

There are also some grains you can pop, like Amaranth, and those grains of rice they make Rice Krispies with, oh, and sorghum and quinoa, and even barley and wheat can all be popped ... well, they don't necessarily "pop" they kinda puff, but they still make a good crunchy snack.

Okay, back to popping corn. How the heck do we make popcorn without a microwave and those little cellophane packets? This is how I make it. (Yes, I learned to make my own popcorn - geeze.) Now, listen up – it's actually pretty easy and foolproof if you follow these steps. *Oooo-kay*?

First, buy a bag of good ol' fashioned popcorn (hint it comes in a bag with hard kernels and is usually found on the same shelf or near where you buy your "microwave" popcorn.)

Once you have your bag of popcorn, grab a 3-quart saucepan, and add three tablespoons of oil to it. Then, add three or four individual popcorn kernels to the oil, and cover the pot with a lid. Heat the oil on medium-high. When you hear the kernels pop (they will hit the top of the lid inside and make a clinking sound – that's your clue that they have popped), add 1/3 cup of popcorn kernels to the pot and create an even layer, enough to cover the bottom of the pan. Put the lid back on the pot and remove the saucepan from heat for 30 seconds; this allows the oil to heat up all the kernels to achieve a near-popping temperature, and all the kernels will pop at about the same time.

Put the saucepan back on the heat. The kernels should begin popping all at once fairly quickly. Once the popping begins gently shake the pan by moving it back and forth over the burner to keep it from burning. When the popping slows down to a few seconds between pops, remove the pan from the heat (don't forget in all your excitement to shut off the stove top burner!) Pour the popped corn into a big bowl and season it to taste (be creative and use butter, garlic, cinnamon, cheese, or any other seasoning of your liking.)

And, there you have it! Delicious popcorn for everyone, or hopefully no one is around, and like me when it comes to popcorn, you can eat it all yourself and be a little piggy. *Yummmmmmeeeeeeeee!*

What You Can Do To Prepare

If and when the poo ever hits the fan, we are going to need as many of the "creature comforts" that we can possibly have during a "not so pleasant" time. And, who doesn't like popcorn? Well, I'm sure there are a lot of people out there who don't ... I just don't personally know of any because it seems like I am always fighting over the popcorn bowl with someone.

So, let's say you are on the move and don't have the luxury of an inside stove top, you can still make a single serving of popcorn over the campfire coals. Just grab a piece of foil about 20 inches long, add a handful of kernels and a teaspoon of oil. Fold the foil over and crimp the open edges. Slide a stick long enough to keep your hand away for the heat, and hold the foil over the coals. The kernels will begin to pop. Once the kernels stop "popping" like with the stove top method, your popcorn is almost ready ... slowly and carefully open the foil ... and then ... "please pass the salt!!" – Just sayin'.

Notes:

Soups On!
Making Something
Out of Nothing

Mm mm soup. I love soup. The first thing that comes to mind when I hear "soup" is cold weather and sipping on a piping-hot cup of tomato soup ... oh, with a melt in your mouth grilled cheese sandwich to go with it. *Mmm, hmm. Yummmeee.*

Did you know that tomato soup; along with chicken noodle and cream of mushroom are the top three most purchased soups in the United States? Well, this little fact got me to thinking that maybe we might want to look into soups a little further as a food source before we are faced with a time when food becomes a little more-scarce or too pricey.

So, what is soup? Well, it comes from the Latin word "*suppa'* which means bread soaked broth. Maybe that is why soup and sandwiches taste so good together ... bread and broth?

As with a lot of food staples of today, soup has a long history dating back to 6000 BC, as a basic sustenance (pause for lesson); sustenance means nourishment, i.e., something that keeps someone or something alive. In a survival situation we may need to know how to make soup for sustenance, so I figured, it would also be a good thing to know a little about the stuff – soup too.

There are two groups of soup; the clear kind and the thick kind. Both types of soup can be made with anything from meat, poultry, fish, fruits and vegetables (yes you heard me right, I said fruits - soup doesn't always have to be hot ya know.) Fruit soups are really pretty easy to make, just steep the fruit; seeds, pits, stems, skins of the fruit and all. The flavor will intensify as it steeps. Heck, I can even make this! Just strain the liquid and chill before serving.

You make most soups by simply combining items like meat and vegetables with stock, juice, water or any other liquid, or sometimes, combine them all. The great thing about soup is, it allows us to experiment with meats, herbs, seasonings, and spices (so make sure to stock up on your spices and herbs in your food supplies.)

Think of this, while one piece of meat may feed a few people served with a side of veggies, imagine how many more it could feed if you took that same piece of meat, put it in to a big pot of beef stock, added some seasonings, herbs and spices, and those veggies. There may even be leftovers for another meal or two.

As a starting point to making your own soup, use leftovers or things you have in your pantry, oh and your creativity. Begin thinking about the things that will be available to us in a poo-hits-the-fan scenario ... and, those things we may not have.

I can remember many times, taking a boring can of soup, and "doctoring it up" by adding a can of chicken or turkey, some herbs and spices and turning it into a great meal ... yes, with bread for dipping of course!

What You Can Do To Prepare

Do you remember the story about "stone soup" or "button soup" (depending on who's telling it)? The story goes something like this; a newcomer comes into town where the town's people are hungry. In the center of town he sets up a campfire and hangs a pot filled with water over the fire. He then places a stone in the pot. Soon the water begins to boil. Intrigued, the town's people inquire as to what he was making. He replies "stone soup," and then suggests an item that would make the "stone soup" even better. Each time the newcomer suggests yet another item that would make the soup better; a resident would promptly go and retrieve it to add to the soup. Ultimately, the ending result was a big pot filled with vegetable soup to share with the town, all made from a stone and water! All it took was teamwork! Oh, and on a survival note, you can actually heat water by taking heated rocks and placing them in the water. Now that is real stone soup! – Just sayin'

Notes:

❧ 9 ❧
Survival Gear

EDC:
What the Heck Is That?

I've been surprised at how many of the more, shall we say, *seasoned* preppers aren't sure what the heck an *EDC* is actually for, or even means. But, who could blame them, or anyone who is trying to learn all those crazy acronyms out there ... like BOB, BOV and GOOD, just to name a few.

For you "less seasoned" or just starting out people, BOB stands for "Bug-Out Bag," BOV for "Bug-Out-Vehicle" and GOOD stands for "Get-Out-Of-Dodge." As for, EDC, it stands for "Every Day Carry." It is either a bag, a wallet or individual items that you want with you e-v-e-r-y d-a-y. These are items truly essential, and that you feel the most secure having with you. You know - items that you practically can't live without?

For a guy's EDC it could be a comb, wallet, pocket knife, laptop, smart phone, and keys. For a mommy, her ECD could be her diaper bag, and in it everything pertaining to her baby's needs, plus some personal items, while away from home. A business person's EDC could have things like a laptop, extra batteries, important documents, their smart phone, maybe an energy bar or two, a bottle of water, you know – all-items-business. And, for working or non-working women – wow, now that is a toughie. I mean, just the thought of what women put in their handbags ... their EDC bag can conger up imagines of the television game show *"Let's Make a Deal"* right? We carry so much stuff in our bags whether we need it or not. "Does anyone have a can opener on them?" ... see where I'm going?

So what does an EDC have to do with survival preparedness? And, why add yet another thing, or things, to an already mounting list of survival needs? Well, the short answer is this, most women are already carrying an EDC bag, and it's usually in the form of their handbag. And for men, the normal things they carry are their EDCs. These items for women and men just have a name. For example, like I mentioned above, mommies may have a diaper bag that serves as their EDC bag and include such things as a wallet, cell phone, multi-tool, band aids and antiseptic cream, cash, granola/energy bars, a bottle of water, a pencil/note pad, a whistle, small manicure kit and a lighter. Not necessarily just the items you would expect in a diaper bag. Say a mommy broke down on the side of the road where there was no cell service, and had to remove, or pry, or loosen something that would at least enable the car to limp to a safe destination instead of just sitting stranded in "nowhere land". She could use that multi-tool in her bag, and then munch on the granola bar and drink her water keep her energy level up.

What do I carry with me? I have a multi-tool, a small adjustable wrench, a mini LED flashlight, a small First-Aid Kit, N95 masks, a small SW/AM/FM radio, some cash, a small makeup bag (don't judge), hair ties, a scarf, a fold up brush, small manicure set, granola/energy bars, a pencil/note pad, a metal pen (which works great as a weapon too by the way), a whistle with compass, my cell phone, a disposable lighter, keys to house and vehicle, dental floss, needles and thread, ear plugs, eye drops, goggles, sunglasses, a paracord key chain, magnesium fire starter and pepper spray. And, that's just in the first section of my bag (just kidding!) I know what you are thinking, "Your bag must be huge!!" But the truth is, all the things I have, plus more, fits in a fanny-pack size bag with a lot of organizer pockets. The items I described are not full-size – we are talking compact here. Notice I said small, mini, tiny, et cetera? I have access to tools, first-aid, eyes, nose, mouth and head protection, and emergency nourishment with me at all times.

What You Can Do To Prepare

You might ask, "Why have an EDC with you when you already have an emergency bag sitting in your vehicle and one at home?" And, that is a great question. The reason is that we are not always near our vehicles or homes. Or, your vehicle could be destroyed or damaged and with it your entire emergency supplies in it. We are talking about items to have with you every day.

Once you realize how little room all these items take up and the huge benefit of having such items with you, I would now hope you will sit down (well you really don't have to sit down, you can stand up, hop on one foot, whatever's comfortable) and make a list of your own items and then start acquiring them.

I can't stress this enough, we never know when a disaster of any kind can strike. It could be the difference between us surviving and ... well, us not surviving (insert the ugly word "death") just by having a few essential items with us at all times – Just sayin'.

Notes:

Paracord:
The Survival Rope

Have you ever given any thought to rope for your emergency disaster supplies? Neither had I, that is, until I needed some rope for a project. I found some in a bucket out in the garage. I never realized how many different types of rope there were, until I began to untangle the bookoodles of twine, nylon cord and string all snaked together like a giant pretzel gone bad. Looking down at the entangled mass I wondered if there was one rope that could work for all my projects and be a great addition to my survival preps too?

The search was on. Now some may or may not agree, but what I found was 550 seven strand paracord, or parachute cord. After a little more research on paracord I purchased some of this manly-man's rope. And, you know what? This stuff is really great. Why? Well first because it weighs next to nothing. I purchased a hundred feet of this rope and it is as light as a feather. Think about if you were caught in a situation where you actually had to carry your survival gear with you ... including the rope. Less weight is always better, right?

Paracord has seven strands, and within each of these strands, there are even smaller filaments, all woven together and covered in a tubular sheath, which makes this rope far stronger than say some of the three strand types of rope on the market. Seven strands have to mean something, right? And, by golly it does (*giggle* who uses that word anymore?) It withstood a 550 pound weight test! (No it wasn't me; it was from the research I did.) What this means, the breaking strength for paracord is ... yep, you guessed it, is 550 pounds! That's pretty darn durable, I'd say. Now, this doesn't mean, you can go swinging on the rope all Tarzan-like - it is not really rated for climbing.

Then there are the color choices. There are hundreds of colors and patterns to choose from! Okay, maybe not hundreds, but a lot - just in case you want to accessorize with your camo (*grin*)! And, speaking of accessorizing, you can use paracord to make a makeshift belt or suspenders, or a shoe string if one broke. Or even tie your hair back with some.

You can also use paracord for grooming aids. Unwind one of the small filaments that make up one of the seven strands inside the paracord to use as dental floss. Or as thread to stitch up a wound. Remember redundancy is paramount in a survival situation, so we need backups for our backups!

How about survival uses? You can use paracord to secure a tent, make a clothes line, tie things down, or secure your emergency go-bag. You could use it to hunt for food by making a snare or a makeshift a bow by tying the paracord to a broken tree branch and then gathering up some long sticks for arrows. And, for fishing, by making a fishing line made from one of the filaments.

Another great thing about paracord is if it gets wet, it dries quickly and won't rot or mildew. That's a really good thing. There is nothing worse than that mildew-y smell. Am I right?

What You Can Do To Prepare

The list for paracord uses could go on and on. But why spoil all the funny and do the work for you? Go get some paracord and start being creative with different uses.

I will share one last use. When researching for more paracord uses this one use grabbed my attention, it said, uh, ... well, you could use it to string up a dear (*giggle* - I think they meant a deer) but I'm sure there could come a time, in a stressful enough situation, where you might be tempted to string up your dear!

Now where is that hubby of mine? Here, dear ... here deary, dear. I want to try something. – Just sayin'.

Notes:

It's Not Easy Being Green:
Learning to Camouflage Yourself

Each weekday morning like clockwork, I used to start my day standing mindlessly at my closet whining about how I didn't have anything to wear, as I aimlessly raked my hands back and forth through the mounds of clothes all aligned like obedient tin soldiers.

For some of you, this decision will be one of the most critical decisions you will make the whole day (scary huh?), and one that could actually make-or-break how the day goes from that point forward.

The same decision-making could hold true during an emergency disaster as well. In emergency preparedness, you have to put just as much thought into your clothing (hopefully more) as you do the items you put in your go-bag. And, thus the topic of camouflage clothing begins.

"Wait, you want me to wear Army clothes?!" I can hear it now. "I look horrible in green!" Yeah, yeah – what I am talking about here is c-a-m-o-u-f-l-a-g-e clothing. And, for the record not everyone who wears camouflage clothing is in the Army ... or military for that matter and not all camouflage clothing is green.

Let's discuss the purpose behind wearing camouflage clothing. The reason the military wears camouflage is so they are undetectable; so they can hide, or blend in when out in the field.

Here's a little lesson on camouflage (I hear your groans), people have used some form of camouflage since the beginning of human civilization - caveman times – as they learned to adapt and blend in with their environment and avoid detection by predators by observing animals We use camouflage every day. In fact, for some of us every morning when we apply our make-up (to hide and conceal imperfections); we try to trick the eye into thinking we have higher cheek bones, longer lashes, and big pouty lips. And with our clothing, we wear body shapers to make our hips look slimmer, push-up bras to … push things up, dark colors and small patterns on our bigger parts and light colors and big patterns on our not so big parts. All of this is applying the camouflage theory of using two basic elements: color and pattern.

The reason for the digital patterns or the abstract or squiggly patterns in military camouflage clothing, is because it makes it visually disruptive, or in other words, the twisty-wavy lines of the camouflage pattern help hide the contour of the body (oh for the day when every piece of clothing were camouflage, right? Sounding better already huh?)

Humans tend to recognize something as a separate object if it has one continuous color – which means a person is much more likely to stand out when wearing a single color than when wearing a jumble of colors. Notice how the woman in the red dress walks into a room and heads turn? Or, the red car on the highway always gets the speeding ticket? Put that same woman in a neutral, like say tan, or patterns and you might not give her a second glance.

Animals use techniques such as surrounding themselves in an environment as their coat/skin coloring to break up their outline, so they don't stick out. They also mimic or try to look like other dangerous animals. Wouldn't it seem to reason that we too would want to use these techniques in a survival situation – to avoid detection from predators, i.e., the "have-nots"?

What You Can Do To Prepare

Consider neutrals for your go-bag and clothing in a "get-the-heck-outta-town" situation. You want to make yourself undetectable – not stand out by wearing colors (for colors think color wheel or rainbow, red, orange, yellow, blue, etc.) Neutrals are tan, beige, drab olive, brown, black; earthy tones. Neutrals; not colors, will always be a safer bet to wear for your survival. And, not to worry darling you will look fabulous in anything … even camo!! - Just sayin'.

Notes:

Shapes and Sizes:
How to Use Camouflage
Techniques for Survival

If, heaven forbid, you find yourself in a "hunted" situation by a human predator, one of the skills you will need to know is "how to camouflage yourself" to avoid detection.

Our brain is actually hard-wired to know shapes specific to humans and will seek these shapes out. For instance, you see a silhouette down the street in a dimly lit area, instantly you know it's a person and not an animal. In a survival situation, should you find yourself being hunted, and the need to hide to avoid detection, albeit in an ally, wooded area, or wherever … the concept is still the same; you need to attempt to break-up your outline.

Going back to the way our brain's work – we know a human has a head, two arms, and two legs. This is elementary. Think back to when you were a child and how you drew a person. Children draw stick people by how their brains perceived them. Stick people. That's right, a head, two arms, and two legs.

Do whatever you can; anything, from sticking branches into your clothing to break up your silhouette (we have seen this done many times by soldiers), to throwing a cover over your head. The idea is to break up the outline of your body and trick the predator's eye.

Remember, Inspector Clouseau, a character in the Pink Panther movies? He was a master at blending in. (Watch a few of the movies, they will be both educational and yes, although a little hokey, entertaining.) In fact, we see the principles of camouflage used a lot in comedy. Even cowboys wore camouflage. The fringe on their leather jackets was to help distort their shape.

We want to avoid detection. Be creative; remember your hunter is looking for a specific shape. Place an irregular object on your head if crouched behind something; it could be as simple as the lid to the trash you are hiding behind (hey, we're taking survival here not fashion.)

Some other tips you might want to remember, is to try to reduce any shine from your skin or from any jewelry you are wearing. Cover all areas of exposed skin, including face, hands, neck, and ears. Use whatever means you can; dirt, charcoal, grease or mud. Use a darker color in areas that stick out more and catch more light (think the areas we usually powder - forehead, nose, cheekbones, chin, and ears). Also, cover other areas, particularly recessed or shaded areas (around the eyes and under the chin) with lighter colors. Be sure to use an irregular pattern – again, kinda like you see the military guys do. (Seeing a pattern here?)

What You Can Do To Prepare

There could be certain situations where some or any of the camouflage techniques we've discussed might be difficult to do, but if you are able to, try to blend in with surrounding colors, patterns, and shapes to avoid detection. This will take some creative thinking on your part – but this is survival we are talking about; namely yours.

If you are wearing white you wouldn't want to hide behind something dark. Try to find like colors. The same holds true for textures and your surroundings. If nothing else try to dirty your clothes if they are light. Hold your arms down close to your body and lock your knees together so you don't have the identifying "arm and leg shape" silhouette of a human — or be "the tree" by holding your arms up in a geisha-girl stance. Or possibly stand behind something like a hanging tree branch or the tassels hanging-down from an awning.

Remember, you want to break up your silhouette any possible way you can. I know ... breaking up is such as hard thing to do. - Just sayin'.

Note:

"Little GTO" – Oldie But Goodie Cars
Having a Reliable Vehicle

Little GTO, you're really lookin' fine
Three deuces and a four-speed and a 389
Listen to her tachin' up now, listen to her why-ee-eye-ine
C'mon and turn it on, wind it up, blow it out GTO
(Ronny and the Daytonas - GTO)

Okay, so this song might be a little before your time (okay ... "a lot" little), but have you ever noticed how a crowd seems to gather around a classic car when it drives up? Muscle cars, like the GTO, Chevelle SS, Road Runner, Mustang, and Mach-I, were all built a long time ago. The appeal of these cars is that they are all made of metal; which means they are solid. And, they are fast.

Today most manufacturers build their vehicles with a bunch of useless pieces of plastic or some sort of plastic composite and microprocessors – a lot of microprocessors. So in essence, we are driving plastic computers on wheels!

I found out the hard way, just what cars are made of these days after someone backed into the front of my (high-end) car. As I got out of the car to check the damage, I thought to myself, "I hope this guy didn't bend the front grille of my car." He didn't. His vehicle totally smashed the daylights out of it. The grille was plastic! Plastic painted to look like shiny chrome. That is when I realized, they don't make cars like they used to. What we get today is genuine plastic burl wood trim, genuine vinyl leather-like seats and, of course the plastic dashboard and vents.

Then, after the plastic came the computer (and sensors). As a little history lesson, (groan, I know) around 1975, vehicles began to come with these new fang-dangled sensors. Since that time, every time something lights up on your dashboard indicating a problem, you have to take it in for service. They hook your car up to a diagnostic machine and read it. Then, presto! $300 and four hours later you drive off, your car is now fixed.

Think about this. What can you do at work, or at home for that matter, without your computer? Not much right? In our home the refrigerator, microwave, oven, washing machine, and dishwasher all have embedded processors in them. And, the same holds true for our vehicle now too. We have gone from a few microprocessors to over 50 in some vehicles, and in others 100. And everything is all tied together!

Now let's say, heaven forbid, some third world country gets a bug up their back-end or some foreign terrorist turned hero propels a nuclear warhead way up into the atmosphere (about 200 miles high) and detonates the weapon which causes an electromagnetic pulse (EMP) over the United States; or at least the better part of it. It will totally wipe out the power grid and communications. And what happens to all those electronic ignition vehicles and those that contain microprocessors? They will immediately be rendered useless.

This is a thought. Maybe we need to start rethinking those pre-1975 *oldie but goodie* cars, and not put so much faith in their electronic (microprocessor-laden) ignition cousins?

Pre-1975 cars had carburetors before the electronic ignition, and were not computerized until the mid-1980s. But by the late 1980s, fuel injection, electronically controlled carburetors, and a rudimentary computer control system were the norm. Which to tell you the truth ... I don't have a clue what all that means except now our cars are rolling computers.

Take the scenario of the EMP strike. Chances are your vehicle's entire electrical system will be totally fried along with the entire power grid for most of our county! An EMP conducts through lines of metal, in other words, it travels through metal ... which means it can travel through antennas on houses, telephone lines, and power lines (above and below ground) see where I am going? Think lines and the EMP is most likely gonna zap it. Look around you. What do you see? Fences, pipes, tracks, sprinkler lines ... all metal. All places an EMP could travel.

Okay, okay, you're probably thinking ... well if there is no power why do I even need a vehicle? The answer, you just *may* want to "get-outta-dodge" to a safe destination, and a vehicle could be an option. You definitely don't want to find yourself in a situation where there is no power and you are stuck some place with no way to get out. (Think mass refugees.)

A reliable vehicle could get you to your safe retreat, or *a safe retreat*, as quickly as possible, before others realize what is happening, by you taking the back roads.

What You Can Do To Prepare

The threat of an EMP attack on our country is bigger than it has ever been. So, this is just one of the many things to consider when preparing for an EMP. You might want to look into an older, pre-1975, mechanical diesel, or gas vehicle for a backup to your "computer on wheels." Unless, of course, you won the lottery; inherited a bunch of money; or are independently wealthy (did I cover everything?) and you can afford to EMP-harden your vehicle. Cha-Ching! – Just sayin'.

Notes:

Mirror, Mirror On the ...
Using a Mirror to Survive

This is going to come as a surprise to some of you women ... but that mirrored compact sitting at the bottom of your purse can actually be more valuable in a survival situation than for that emergency nose and forehead powdering.

We know, or should know, how important it is to have shelter, emergency water and food, and a way to protect your belongings in a disaster situation, but how about what to do if you find yourself stranded – and in need of rescuing?

A mirror could be the key to a successful rescue simply by following some general guidelines. Oh, and no, size does not matter - you can use something as tiny as the mirror on the end of a lipstick tube to something as big as the rearview mirror off your disabled vehicle. The flash from a two-inch diameter compact-mirror (the size most women carry); in ideal conditions, and during the day could potentially be seen from almost 100 miles away – yes I said one hundred miles away. Sure that is the extreme, but the general rule of thumb is about 10 miles, and even that is still pretty far.

You might be thinking that this "distress signal" will only work in the daylight, and luckily you would be wrong. It's true, a mirror works best in good sunlight, but it can also work on overcast days too. A mirror can reflect on almost any light source, headlights, a flashlight, a candle or, even the bright moonlight, the key is to aim it at the light source correctly. The bright flash created will show your whereabouts even in densest of areas and rugged landscape.

So let's say you accidentally drop your mirror or it somehow gets broken (who knew it would break when you threw it down in frustration?) Just pick up one of the pieces, (remember size doesn't matter) to use, just be careful not to cut yourself while holding the broken pieces– or you will create a second disaster.

If for some unforeseen reason, you find yourself without your compact mirror (oh the shame of it all!), there are other objects that might work just as well. You could use the rearview mirror off a car; a CD (the disc), aluminum foil, the bottom of aluminum can or even jewelry. Be creative. Women are creatures attracted by shiny objects. If it shines – more than likely it reflects too!

So, here's how to use your mirror for something other than applying powder to your face (women). Hold the mirror with your fingertips along the edges of the mirror with the back facing you and the shiny (reflective) part facing away from you (for easier handling, you may want to break the powder base off the compact. I know … I know.) Turn the mirror towards the Sun (or light source.) Hold your opposite arm out stretched in front of you with your palm facing towards you – then move the mirror until you are able to see a bright spot of light on the palm of your outstretched hand. Now, move the mirror closer to your eye or forehead. Locate the target that you would like to signal to, and move the bright spot of light from the palm of your hand towards the target by tilting the mirror.

If the Sun is setting, hold out your outstretched hand and form a V shape with two fingers. Then, sight the mirror reflection on the V; now move the V and the reflection towards the target at the same time.

This is a practiced skill. So along with all the other things you are practicing, add mirror signaling to the list.

What You Can Do To Prepare

A mirror is one of the most overlooked emergency items we can have in our go-bags, and yet it is so small and versatile (like using it to start a fire for instance.) Sure you can buy a signal mirror that actually has a hole in the middle of the reflector to make the targeting process a lot easier, but even so, we also need to understand and know, for redundancy sake, how to use a plain ol' mirror or a shiny object as well.

So, the next time you check your hair in the car rearview mirror, remind yourself that in an emergency, the reflection you really want to see looking back at you, is not you ... but help on the way. – Just sayin'.

Notes:

❧ 10 ❦
Sustainable Living

Kinda Seedy Subject:
Seed Vaults

So, let's say there is a catastrophic event … a not so good one, (not that any catastrophic event would be good), like say … uh, the end of the world *as we know it* type of event. Destruction everywhere, mass causalities, air and water pollution, nationwide power outages, - you know, like in a split second we are thrown back to the way people lived 200 years ago … and have to pick up the pieces and start over.

Where will you get food when you've used up all your food storage? Trust me your food stockpile is only going to last so long. You can't plant an MRE, right? Or plant a can of beanie weenies. And, you definitely can't plant a bag of flour, sugar, coffee, tea, or anything else for that matter and hope to get more food storage.

So, what is the remedy for replenishing your food supplies? The Answer is a seed vault. A seed vault is a little known secret that apparently the government and other countries are good at keeping a secret. These countries, including our own, are hoarding every type and variety of fruit, vegetable, and plant seeds currently known in the world. And, why do you think these countries are doing this? "Because they are smarter than us?" you ask. Uh … nope, well, yeah, but in a weird kind of way. They are saving seeds under the guise of "preserving" these seeds. You know like – scientifically saying, "Too bad we don't have a dinosaur embryo so we can see what a dinosaur really looked like way back when."

More and more seed vaults are popping up all over the place, like the *Native Seeds* in Tucson, Arizona; the *Ambrose Monell Cryo Collection* in New York City; the *Millennium Seed Bank Project* in West Sussex, UK, and *Wakehurst Place* near London. But the most notorious MacDaddy vault of them all is the *Svalbard Global Seed Vault* tucked away on the island of Spitsbergen in the Barents Sea near the Arctic Ocean in the country of Norway (not surprising is the fact that the investors for *Svalbard Global Seed Vault* are the likes of the Bill and Melinda Gates Foundation, the Rockefeller Foundation, Monsanto Corporation, Syngenta Foundation, and the Government of Norway – you know … *moneyed* people.)

Now I appreciate science just as much as the rest of you (well not that much really), but in my opinion, this sounds a little like … "If something terrible were to happen to our planet, let's make sure that we have the means to rebuild." (Paraphrasing of course.) And, at first glance that looks pretty noble … until you realize, "Hey wait a minute, they have all the seeds!" And who do you think will have all the power? Remember: "He who rules the food rules the world!"

So as usual, this got me to thinking, how does someone like I used to be, whose meals were primarily out of a box (sometimes a to-go box from the drive-thru window, sometimes delivered to my doorstep), even going to begin to know how to gather seeds?

A lot of questions began to pop into my little pea brain. First, I wondered what that spot was on my shirt and how it got there. But I digress. Okay, back to the seeds. I wondered if I could save seeds from like say, the sliced tomato on my hamburger, or from the cucumber in my salad, or even from produce I got at the grocery store.

Come to find out, there is more to seeds then I thought. You first need to know about the different types of seeds before learning what to do with them. For instance, if the seeds came from fruit or vegetables at the local farmers market, there's a good chance the seeds you would be dealing with are heirloom seeds – you know like granny-maw used, and most likely you would be able to save the seeds from these fruits and vegetables.

But what about grocery store produce? Now, that's a bird of a different color (or whatever the heck that saying is.) Most, if not all, the produce found in grocery stores are grown with hybrid seeds – two different varieties combined to make a third variety; and genetically altered to make them plumpier (it could be a word), the juiciest and more colorful – which are all pleasing to the eye. Unfortunately, the success rate of these seeds reproducing is not the best, and can actually revert back to an earlier variety of either parent variety, or not reproduce at all. Oh yeah, and also grocery store produce may also come from another type of seed … a darker more sinister seed type which involves a powerful cartel of seed companies and laboratories – think Monsanto, (cue the sinister organ music) called GMO seeds, or genetically modified seeds – now think Frankenstein. These seeds are created with chemicals for "commercial growing" – and are really not good for us.

So how do you remember if the seed is an heirloom or heritage seed? Think, little white-laced hankie being passed down year after year from one person to another – that's heirloom. Think vanilla and chocolate ice-cream swirled cone - that's hybrid.

And those seed packets you buy at the store? Unfortunately those are "consumer products" (products made for one time use only) and most of them manufactured from the cartel ... er ... big seed companies. And, like most consumer products, these seeds are usually hybrids; genetically altered with an inability to reproduce – which means you get one shot with them (that is if they even take at all). With heirloom seeds, you can save the seeds year-to-year. And, with some types you can even save them for years.

What You Can Do to Prepare

Heirloom seeds will be your best bet for long-term seed storage. Make sure to pick the hardiest of fruits and vegetables grown with heirloom seeds to save for your own seed vault. To store the seeds properly, make sure the seeds are totally dry first. Then seal them in an envelope with the date and variety, and place them in a cool, dry, dark place. Make a habit of saving seeds as you are preparing a piece of fruit or a vegetable for a meal or snack. You usually don't eat the seeds after all. In fact, I don't recall anyone saying, "These seeds are so yummy." Well, Okay there are a few yummy seeds, like pomegranates ... details! - Just sayin'.

Notes:

Now You See It – Now You Don't: Making a Liquid Predator Repellent Fence

If you have not already done so, you might want to seriously consider creating a garden, albeit a full acre plot, planter boxes, raised beds or a food forest. In the not so distant future, the food you grow could be the only food you have to eat. Why? Well, with inclement weather ever-changing; such as droughts and torrential rains, crops getting damaged by freezes, hail and bug infestations, and the cost of gas making it costly to ship, fresh fruits and vegetables – food could become too costly to buy. So the sooner we plant … the better.

At first, for me a former city girl, I hated the thought of getting my hands dirty. But guess what? Those days are over. I want to eat and to do that, I have to get my hands dirty – under the nails and all (ugh!) Or, wear gloves, which I do that too – a lot.

So, we can all agree, we like to eat, right? Hmm? I said, right?! Well then get yourself a garden "how-to" book at your local bookstore that suits you and your family's needs and start planning that garden.

Heck urbanites grow veggies and fruits on their patio or roof top even in the midst of all that concrete, asphalt, and glass. Why not plant herbs in a window box or a small garden and some fruit or nut trees in your backyard? You might even join with other like-minded people and grow a vegetable garden within your community; but take note; you also need rules, guidelines, restrictions, and procedures (whatever you choose to call them) set in place in advance addressing who gets to partakes in the goods. Remember the story of the Little Red Hen?

No matter which type of garden you decide on, there will be natural pests who will wait until you have done all the work and then jump in and start eating. And I mean chowing down eating. There are three categories of these garden pests; domestic, wild, and insect, and each is unique to the specific regions of your garden. So, along with learning all-things-gardening, you will also want to learn about pests and how to combat them as well (I hear your groans).

The number one menace in my garden is a deer, then comes rabbits and of course insects. Now granted, an insect can do some damage, but compared to a deer, Katie-bar-the-door, hands down the deer win. As frustration set in for me, I wondered how the heck I was going to stop these beautiful creatures from consuming my entire garden? The quest was on! Find a deer repellent. What I initially found was a lot of comments from people who said, "I did this," and "I did that." Everyone had their remedies. But the one remedy that stood out from the others was a liquid fence (of course I find this after incurring the cost of putting up a six-foot wire fence, which had only served to allow the deer to engage in aerial acrobatics as they leaped over it.) I must say a liquid fence sounded intriguing – but I needed to do more research.

Now, these liquid fence-type products that you can buy in stores or online are … well, *reeeeally* pricey; well for me. And, besides where would we get these products, if and when, the poo ever hit the fan? I needed to find an alternative and one I could continue to use no matter what. And she shoots, she scores! Yes! There is a homemade alternative to these store-bought products! So, I set out to make some. WARNING: The stuff I made stinks to high-heavens, so don't get it on your hands or you will be repelling more than animals!

The recipe I used, called for one egg, five garlic cloves (or two and a half teaspoons of minced garlic), five gallons of water, and five one-gallon containers (I used discarded milk jugs.) Luckily, I had everything I needed.

To make the liquid fence, you crack open an egg and put it into one of the gallon containers. Then, fill the container with water and kinda swirl it around. Divide the egg and water mixture equally into all five containers, so that each container has a little of the egg water mixture. Now, fill the containers the rest of the way up with fresh water and place one crushed clove of garlic (or a half a teaspoon of minced garlic) in each container. Sit the containers out for several days – in the sunlight preferably. Once the concoction has fermented (cooked in the Sun) it is ready for use (oh, don't worry... you will know.) *Wooo-weee!* This recipe gives a whole new twist to rotten eggs!

To use your homemade liquid fence, take one of the containers at a time, and pour the contents on and around plants, and areas you don't want deer or rabbits to eat, or go near. Oh, and don't worry the awful smell will dissipate as it dries and you won't smell it ... but the deer and rabbits sure will! The downside to liquid fence is it is not a permanent solution. After it rains, the plants require reapplication, so keep a couple empty gallon jugs around – well actually five empty gallon jugs so you can make more as needed.

What You Can Do To Prepare

We need to really think about our basic needs and how we are going to achieve each of these needs before something bad happens. But, we might also want to consider how we are going to protect these basic needs. Gardens are not foolproof; they take planning and nurturing to create a lasting food source ... so plan now.

Since using my homemade liquid fence, no two-legged or four-legged predators have eaten from my garden ... except me! – Just sayin'.

Notes:

Gardening:
It's Not Just Putting a Seed
In the Ground

We can have all the food storage in the world – okay maybe not the world – but nonetheless, a lot of food in our storage pantries, but when the poo-hits-the-fan, there will come a time when all that food storage is gone – all gone. Whether the food is consumed by us, bugs, spoilage, damaged, stolen; whatever, there will be no more running out to the store or ordering more online. So, as with anything and everything in preparedness, the number one rule is (or if not number one, at least it is close to the top of the list of rules), you need back-ups for your back-ups.

For those who are new to preparedness and don't understand what "having backups for your backups" means, let me explain. Say you have a great pair of sandals you are going to wear for a weekend picnic event. What you didn't know beforehand was that the event also included a hike. If, you would have put a pair of boots in the car as a backup you would have been fine. Or, say you were hosting a party and you burnt the dessert with no time to recreate another before guests arrive, you grab some graham crackers, and break them apart, heat some chocolate chips in the microwave with a little coconut oil added, stir in some marshmallows and you have an instant dessert! You had a backup! It's all about contingency planning for *woulda, shoulda, coulda's* that can happen. This includes our food stores.

My first attempt at planting heirloom seeds was, eh … shall we say, not so good. None of the seeds I planted in the garden took, or at least most of them didn't for some reason or another (head hung in shame.) Thankfully, I had also purchased seedlings from a reputable nursery and when I planted them in the garden, they flourished ... really flourished (big grin).

So in my infinite wisdom, I decided I would buy more heirloom seeds, and use some of the seeds I saved from last year's harvest, and grow my own seedlings. I spent weeks and weeks nurturing the little fellows (my seedlings) in my greenhouse; from seed and soil, watching as each seed stuck its little head out, as it reached out for the Sun (at least I think it was their head?) I talked to each one of the seedlings as if talking to a preschooler, encouraging and coaching them along the way. Then, the big day came for them to put on their big boy/girl plant pants and be placed out into the great expanse (the garden). I gingerly took each out of their planting crib and hand-planted them in the ground, one at a time – all three hundred of them. Yes *reeaaalllyy*.

Later, I stood back ogling at the wonders of them all. Each happy healthy plant - superior to the seeds I had planted in the ground the year before.

I "companion-planted" too; which means I put trap plants that attract bugs next to all the other plants, not wanting to use any pesticides, and let the good bugs battle it out with the bad ones, leaving my prize vegetable plants alone. I also planted in a random pattern, "some here and some over there" to avoid smorgasbord-type rows of plants. (Planting in rows is like laying out a buffet for a bug – they can just go down the rows eating away – so I make them work for their food!)

I hung the snow and snap peas - already reaching high to the sky like balloons filled with helium, up on fence trellis. I was *soooo* proud of their accomplishments. And, this before they produced a thing!

As I came out into the garden the next morning, anxious to see how my little pupils were doing, horrified, I saw my snow and snap peas on the ground, broken off at the base of their stems. At first, I chalked it up to not being careful and somehow snapping the stems as I placed them on the trellis. Not wanting to be defeated, I pulled the few "stragglers" I had left in the greenhouse and plant them to take the place of the fallen heroes.

The next day I went out to look at the peas to see how these new recruits were doing. *Agggghhh!* They too were lying on the ground next to their fallen brothers. Dang it!

Well, after a little research on my part, I found out that the culprit to killing off my peas was not me, but a cutworm. They aren't really a worm, but the larvae of caterpillars that hide in the soil by day and come out in the dark (like little sneaks) to feed on plants (cowards). But, in learning about the cutworm, I also found out that I could make a simple barrier to keep the darn things (said with as much love as I could muster up) away from my plants. I could make a collar around the plants by cutting cardboard paper towel rolls (or toilet paper rolls) into 2" pieces and putting them around the plant stems. Some people wrap tin foil around the stems to protect them too.

What You Can Do To Prepare

Think about this. Even though I initially had happy, healthy seedlings in the ground, if the poo had hit the fan, and bugs had eaten these plants, I would have lost a lot of the food I was counting on as backups for my food storage. Things happen.

My suggestion would be since we probably will not have access to computers, if and when the poo hits the fan, is to get a good reference book for your survival library on gardening, and bugs. (Might I suggest the *Secret Garden of Survival: How to Grow a Camouflage Food Forest*, by Rick Austin, I heard it's really good – smile (disclosure he is also my husband).

Not only is it important that we know how to grow from seeds and harvest what we sow, but we also need to learn what kind of "thieves" can wipe out our garden food source in the dark of the night; four-legged and two-legged. - Just sayin'.

Notes:

❧ 11 ❧
Finance

Garage Sale:
Who the Heck Sells their Garage?

When I see garage sale or yard sale signs, I instantly think "good stuff" (and ... sometimes, "really" good stuff) cheap. And, depending on where you live, you can get some of those items new or at least practically new – slightly worn or gently used. Now, I know what some of you may think, because I thought the same thing, "I'm not digging through someone else's junk!" I will admit, the first couple of times I went to one of these sales, it *was* pretty weird rummaging through people's personal items. But after realizing that the owners put the items out to get rid of them, and after scoring a few awesome deals – I got over it ... real fast.

I can't tell you all the great things I've gotten at garage sales – new hiking boots, military-style ponchos, several cast iron skillets, a grinder, a vacuum sealer and so on and so forth – all new mind you – and cost me next to nothing too. I mean that literally. To me, it's not a deal if it is over $10, and most times, I keep it down to one or two dollars.

Before moving to our homestead, I was getting pretty darn good at finding great prep stuff – cheap! I would map out my Saturday morning strategy by using the internet and the newspaper, and then go to homes that ... well, had a higher income base than I did and, who wanted to get rid of those gifts received from holidays or birthdays that they were never going to use or possibly already had one or multiple of. You know, the homes where the people who lived in them would never be caught dead returning an item to a store? So, instead, they waited until their community had their annual garage sale and use that opportunity to get rid of their stuff. My gain! Again, let me stress that most of the things I purchased were brand-new, some still in the box or original packaging.

All those ex-military enthusiasts, ex-camping enthusiasts, un-ambitious or wanna-be gourmet cooks, who at first, thought it would be a fun hobby, now wanted to get rid of all that stuff.

Garage sales were my preparedness gear salvation early on. I had a running survival wish list, and would go "treasure hunting" (my term of endearment for garage sales). I have found things I didn't even think of or have on my list! Like the 20 gallon solar water bag from an ex-camping enthusiast for $3. Think about it, if you don't have access to hot water for some reason during a disaster, you can fill that puppy up, sit it (or hang it) out in the Sun and in a very short-order you have hot water to wash you and other things with. That shower wasn't on my list, but for $3 new in the box, it had my name all over it! See what I mean? Garage sales are a great and inexpensive way to acquire preparedness items.

I was pretty picky too when it came to making deals on items too. If I have to spend a lot of time fixing it up or cleaning it, I'll take a pass on it. My mission is not to spend money and fix something up too. I want the best deal, for the least amount of money. Ah, the American Dream!

You can also find great preps at farm auctions and estate sales. They are great sources for tools, shelving, and canning jars. And, then there is the internet and websites like e-bay and Craigslist you may want to consider too.

What You Can Do To Prepare

The saying "One man's junk is another man's treasure" sure rang true for me when I was just starting out on my preparedness journey. Things are expensive and if I could get a deal, then I was all about it. The economy is not as it was. People need money and we preparedness-minded people need survival items. It's a beautiful thing! A match made in heaven!

Now let's all say it together ... "Excuse me, would you take a dollar for this?" – Just sayin'.

Notes:

All That's Left Is A Band Of Gold: Holding On To Your 24k Gold Jewelry

Have you heard those commercial ads on television or on the radio; you know the ones that shout out to you to "Bring us your solid gold, broken, no longer used, jewelry and we will give you cash!" ... well, something like that. Looking down into my jewelry box, all I saw was a bunch of 24k gold pieces of bent and battered rings, knotted and clasp-less chains and orphan charms. "Why would they want this old stuff?" I wondered.

I soon learned that the reason these companies want your gold, is because more and more people are putting their money into gold as an investment over concerns our currency here in the United States is not faring so well. Gold is gold, whether it's in the form of gold bullion, ingot, coin, bracelet, or charm; if it's 24k it is gold and these companies what it. That includes all my unused jewelry that they could melt down.

There is also talk about using gold as a new form of currency in the not so distant future. In fact, did you know that ten states in our nation, have already initiated bills into legislation that would allow those specific states to use gold; and silver, as legal tender? To date, Georgia, Montana, Missouri, Colorado, Idaho, Indiana, New Hampshire, South Carolina, Utah, and Washington have proposed legislation to include gold and silver as acceptable currency forms. What this could mean is that all monetary transactions could eventually be in gold or silver (and we thought our handbags were heavy before!) It, hasn't become law yet, but think about it, why turn your gold jewelry over to some shyster; who by the way, is probably going to try to rip you off, when you can hang on to your gold, and, when our dollar finally takes its last bow, we will have portable wealth in the form of our jewelry. Yay us!

For those of you who didn't pay attention in history class (yeah me, neither) our United States Constitution reads in part: Article I, Section 10, "No State shall ... make anything but gold and silver coin a tender in payment of debts." Hmm, what happened? What happened was the "Federal Reserve Note." In 1973 the gold standard changed and currency became "fiat" money and its value is now controlled by, yep you guessed it, the Federal government.

Some have even argued that fiat money has no backing and would be entirely worthless, except that the Government has persuaded us to use it and accept it as if it had worth – go figure. (Wonder how much I can get for a rock?)

Another benefit to our 24k gold jewelry is that it would be handled differently by the Government then say, gold bullion, bars, or coins (knock on wood.) To date, jewelry has never been confiscated by the Government, unlike with the "Gold Act of 1933," when they confiscated all privately owned gold bullion and coins ... at a cost below market price.

What You Can Do To Prepare

So, the next time you choose a piece of gold jewelry to go with an outfit, look at it as money in the bank ... well money in your jewelry box because it could very well be our future buying power. Keep in mind, we are only referring to 24k gold jewelry (99.9% gold purity); the highest standard of gold, opposed to 22k, 18k, 14k, or 10k;

which all contain some amount of copper, silver, or palladium in them.

And, when buying gold jewelry, know with confidence, you are making a stable investment in not only your style, but your future! – Just sayin'.

Notes:

❧ 12 ❧
Survival Skills

This Little Light Of Mine:
Blacking Out Your Windows
For Safety and Survival

Most of us consider draperies; sometimes called drapes (*cringe* ... drape is something you do, draperies is an object ... but I digress), or window blinds, more as a decorative touch to our home, then for functionality. At night we close our mini blinds, shades, or draperies for privacy only to open them back up in the morning. And, for the most part the window treatments work well for their intended purpose – keeping people from seeing into the house.

Now let me ask you this, "Have you ever given any thought to the light shining out from around the windows of your house?" If not, as a little experiment, drive down the street of your neighborhood at night and look up at the houses. In each house where there is a light on, and the window treatments are closed, you can see the light coming out from around the closed draperies or blinds. Even with "sheers" (those see through window treatments), you can see movement from the light shining through even if you can't make out the people or the contents of the house clearly.

So what can we do to eliminate any light coming from our house windows at night when we find ourselves in a grid-down situation where there was no electricity, or if and when the poo-hits-the fan and we don't want people knowing anyone is at home? You may want to consider opaque window coverings. "*Opaaaaa* – what coverings?" you ask. Opaque window treatments keep light from penetrate through. Think hotel room draperies, when you

254

close opaque draperies you are standing in pitch dark, if you don't turn on a lamp light first that is.

Imagine this scenario. It's nighttime. Disaster has struck and the streets are dark, in fact everything is dark – the whole city is pitch-black. No lights anywhere. Predators (looters) are out in force casing each neighborhood for homes with any sign of light that would signal those who may have generators, food, water, and possibly weapons. Innocently, you light a candle thinking you are being stealthy with such a tiny amount of light, but that small flicker shines like a beacon in the darkness for anyone from the outside to see ... and, signals to others where you are thereby making you a huge target.

Having a way to blacken-out your windows might be something you want to consider for your preparedness plan, if you are planning on staying put during an emergency event, or because of some unforeseen circumstance that requires you stay in. One option you might want to consider is blackout opaque window film. This film totally blacks out the window and does not let any sunlight in. It's applied directly over the window panes of your home. Then when the poo hits the fan there is no scurrying around to cover windows.

Another option is opaque or black-out draperies. But be forewarned, there are very few window draperies that can completely prevent direct sunlight from penetrating the window – but they would prevent light from coming out from the windows from the inside at night, which is your goal in the first place.

Drapery liners placed with existing draperies can give you privacy and completely darken a room. There are also roll shades on the market that claim to block out all the light as well. But unless the shades are actually fastened to the window frame they still might let light in through the sides. And, I have also heard of using black-out type fabric used on movie sets. Buy the material and make the size window coverings for your windows. Then, have the panels ready to put up in an emergency; fastening the panels to window frames using Velcro.

And lastly, there is glass paint for windows. This seems a little more involved than hanging draperies, but hey, it would definitely do the job!

What You Can Do To Prepare

These options are in no way meant as your only choices. Again, as with a lot of our preparedness preps, creativity can play a huge roll in what decision we make. Black, heavy-duty plastic commercial-grade trash bags, black felt, black tarps – whatever you decide, just remember to check outside at night for any light leaks. If you should see any light coming from the windows after utilizing your black-out treatments, you may want to consider using an opaque duct tape to cover any glaring cracks.

Keep this thought in mind when deciding on your best light eliminating option; - *even the smallest light shines in the dark.* – Just sayin'.

The Fire Starter:
How to Start a Fire without Matches

Do you know how to start a fire? Not, have you ever started a fire. Heck, if that were the case, I'd be the first one to raise my hand! I once pre-heated my oven after accidentally dropping a plastic spatula inside! (Don't ask. I digress.) I'm actually referring to making fire for a survival situation, without matches or a lighter. And, I will tell you right here and now, starting a fire requires every ounce of patience you have and then some. It is not like being at home and flicking your fancy candle lighter and presto your candle is lit. It is a skill, a major skill.

So on to different methods for making a fire. Keep in mind; all these methods need some sort of tinder; which is little pieces-parts of stuff like wood shavings, dried grass, lint, or small twigs to make a nest out of (think bird's nest). You will also need some bigger twigs, sticks, wood to make a woodpile.

The first option is with magnesium and a flint block. If you have these, grab them out of your go-bag and go outside away from trees and bushes – like in your driveway. After you have made your little nest o' tinders, take your knife and scrape a pile of magnesium shavings on top of the tinder nest. Then, strike a spark off the flint with your knife. The magnesium will ignite and hopefully start a flame in the tinder. This is where the patience part comes in. Most times the magnesium will not ignite on the first attempt, or even the second or the third. Don't give up, keep striking. Once you see that glorious glow of ember and the tinder begins to smoke, save the happy dance for later and gently blow into the tinder nest until the fire catches and then, place the tinder nest down into your woodpile. You did make the woodpile ... didn't you?

Now, if it is a sunny day, and you don't have magnesium and a flint block, you can also use a magnifying glass. If you don't a magnifying glass either, look around for a piece of broken glass or even your eye glasses would work – that is if you don't need them to see what you are doing! Anything that is reflective of the Sun will work. With your tinder nest made and wood already gathered and stacked, take the glass, and angle it with the Sun over the tinder. It will eventually begin to smoke. Like with the flint, gently blow on the tinder to help it burn, and then place it in the woodpile.

If you can't find a piece of glass or don't have a flint block hopefully you have a radio or flashlight in your go-bag. Remove the 9-volt or the couple of D, C or AA batteries from the device. Again, have your tinder nest and woodpile ready. You will also need a piece of steel wool ... okay, let me stop here for a minute, after reading this if there is anything mentioned so far that you do not have in your go-bag, make a mental note or write it down and add it to your bag. Nuf said, back to fire starting. Pull off a piece of the steel wool and kinda pull it apart keeping it together, just make it loose metal rope. Touch the steel wool to both charges on the 9 volt battery or stack two of your D, C, or AA batteries on top of one another and touch the steel wool to each end. The steel will start to burn. Place the piece of steel wool on your tinder nest to light it and then place it in the woodpile. (Oh, be sure to store the steel wool and any extra batteries separately to avoid a fire in your go-bag! Puts a whole new spin on putting fire under your feet huh?)

Now as in all situations, things do not always go as planned, and practiced, and if, for some reason you aren't able to get to your go-bag, there is still a method you can use to make fire. Find yourself a stick; as straight as possible, and make a point at one end (this is where a knife will once again come in handy and why it is the number one survival tool. If you don't have one, just scrape the end of the stick on something rough, like a rock, to make a point.) Now look for a flat piece of wood (if you can't find one use tree bark). Cut, or make a little groove into the flat piece of wood and place the stick between the palms of your hands. Position the stick point into the groove of the wood (it may help by putting a little tinder in the groove too.) Rub your hands back and forth, rolling the stick really fast between your palms; making sure that the point of the stick and the flat piece of wood stay in contact with one another. After a while (sometimes a very, very, very, long while), the wood will begin to heat up and make a little ember. Once you see the ember of the tinder, blow on it and put it in your tinder nest and then into the woodpile.

You can also use a Vaseline covered cotton ball for the tinder. In fact, I'd suggest taking a little container and putting a few of these little jewels in it and put in your go-bag. Take the Vaseline coated cotton ball and kinda open it up to expose the insides. Then, begin whatever method is right for the circumstance to make your fire. Once the cotton ball catches fire, place it in your tinder nest and then on the woodpile.

What You Can Do To Prepare

Fire making is a skill that will not only keep you warm, but it can assist in cooking a meal, signal for help, add some light in darkness, and protect you from predators. And, like all preparedness skills you need redundancy. So make sure you practice with different methods and different types of tinder.

Now, come on babe (help me) light my fire. Sorry couldn't resist! – Just sayin'.

Notes

TEOTWAWKI:
What the Heck Does It Mean?

TEOT-WA-WKI.

TEO-T-WAW-KI.

TEOT-WAWK-I.

How do you even pronounce this word? The answer, it depends on who you were to ask. I've hear it pronounced *ti.at.wak.i* or *tea-ought-walk-ee* ... or some say ... "It's not pronounced any way it's an acronym" or "I don't have a clue." I guess it is like asking someone how to make chocolate chip cookies! You are going to get a bazillion different ways.

TEOTWAWKI is in fact an acronym, and stands for "the end of the world as we know it" which, by the way, can mean any number of things. It is a life disruption by an event that alters our everyday lifestyle. It doesn't literally mean the "end of the world," as a lot of people misinterpret it to mean. Think Hurricane Katrina. That was a TEOTAWKI event for those who lived through it and experienced it. Their lives will never be the way they once were ... never, ever. Everything about their existence has changed. Sure their homes may now be restored, and businesses are back up and running, but you can't un-ring the bell of the sights, sounds, and destruction these people have lived through.

We have all probably experienced a TEOTWAWKI, or two, in our lifetime and not even realized it. TEOTWAWKI can mean a loss of job, a loss of a loved one or even something near and dear to us. Again, it is the end of the world as *you* once knew it.

For preparedness-minded people the term TEOTWAWKI refers to a future catastrophic event (my "poo-hits-the-fan"). You never know what can happen or when, but we do know that whatever and whenever, it will never be the way it once was.

There is another acronym you may hear and want to understand a little more too. It is WTSHTF, and means "when the poo (okay the "S" word) hits the fan" or "when the $hit hits the fan." You know, when all heck breaks loose? I like to clean mine up a little and say "when the poo hits the fan" (WTPHTF) – it just sounds a little more eh, lady-like don't cha think?

There can also be as many WTSHTF scenarios as TEOTWAWKI scenarios. Some of the more common ones circulating today are societal collapse, dollar devaluation, economic collapse, natural disasters, man-made disasters, an act of terrorism, an EMP, cyber-attack, and a possible foreign invasion (and don't think that can't happen), each of these has different priorities and might need different plans of action.

So how do you prepare for a TEOTWAWKI event – or when the poo hits the fan? Like the saying goes, "You plan for one you plan for all." Just as you would for any disaster; have your basic needs of food and water at the ready, medical supplies, and the knowledge of how to use the medical supplies, a safe place to shelter in or a safe destination to go to, and, a way to protect yourself and belongings. All of these items make-up the foundation of survival.

Once you put these key areas in place, you can then focus on different scenarios and build from there. For instance, you might require a different plan for hurricane disaster preparedness then say a flood preparedness plan, and so on and so forth.

What You Can Do To Prepare:

As you watch and/or listen to the news, and world events that are going on around you, and you hear of a disaster; natural or man-made somewhere in the world, think about what you would need in that event that would help you to better survive as if you were actually in that disaster. "NGYHG" (*Now Get Your Hiney Going*) – Just sayin'.

Notes:

Making a List and Checking It Twice: Making a Survival Preparedness List

Emergency preparedness can get very overwhelming to a person just starting out. Not to worry though, all preparedness-minded people have gone through it. Once you realize that nobody will be 100 percent prepared; and I mean nobody, for every single disaster or catastrophic event that may come our way your anxiety level should come way down.

Focus first on your needs, then start to prioritize. Forget about what you haven't done, don't have yet, can't get, or will never have. It will all fall into place soon enough. My suggestion as to how to start is to make a list.

Take out a piece of paper and something to write with and just as you would make a list to take with you to the grocery store, or before going on a vacation trip, or for errands you need to run, the same holds true for survival preparation – you need to start with a list.

Begin with the most basic needs and work out from there. They are as follows:

Food

Water

Shelter

Protection

First-Aid

Warmth

There, you see? You have already started your list.

Now, think of all the different situations, and scenarios common to your region, such as; are you in a hurricane or tornado prone area? If, so, how long could you expect to be without power during and after an event such as these? How much of any given item you would need to sustain you for that event? Just work your way down the list for each of the basic needs. It will help you begin to think more clearly about your environment and your specific needs by taking the time to make a list.

Keep in mind that everyone's needs are different, there will be some similarities like water and food, but we all live in different regions of the country and have different resources. So focus on what is best for your survival. Take for instance, someone who lives in an area where there are hurricanes would not require the same survival supplies as someone who lives in blizzard country. Think specifically about warmth, water, sleep, and food as it pertains to you. Do you need alternative power such as a generator? How about fuel? How much fuel?

After a while, you will understand the necessity of certain items that at first might have seemed a little foreign to you, such as a fire starting kit.

As you learn more and more about self-reliance and what can happen in any number of disaster situations, your list will begin to grow into sub-lists. Yes, you heard right, I said sub-lists. You will find as you continue to educate yourself in survival prep that your list will start to branch off into more specific areas (this is a good thing.)

You may have initially put a tent on your first list then move it to a sub list for shelter then add other necessities that would go with a tent, such as tarps.

Once you have you basic needs written down, you may want to turn your attention to basic survival skills next, and make a list for such skills as making fire, building a shelter, finding food and water and, how to administer first-aid.

What You Can Do To Prepare

You can build a strong foundation for your skills, as well as for your survival supplies, by learning what items you need (not want), and what instruction is necessary for your survival.

And ... there you have it, the secret to preparing for any disaster ... a list. Now getta writin'! – Just sayin'.

Notes:

Star Light – Star Bright:
Using Your Body as a Compass for Survival

Did you know that you don't need a compass to know which direction you are heading? Of course in a perfect world, I would hope that you do have one packed in your emergency go-bag for when the need does arise, but if for some unforeseen reason you find yourself sans compass; or even go-bag, you can always get an idea of which direction you are heading by simply using ... your body and nature as a guide.

"And how the heck do you use your body as a compass?" you ask. Well, think of it this way. If you were lying down on your stomach, arms stretched out, your head would be north, your feet south, your right side would be east and your left side would be west. And, standing up it would be the same, your head (or in front of you) is north, south is behind you, east is to your right and west to your left. This never changes. The only thing that changes is where you are looking and what direction you are moving towards.

We all know, or should know that the Sun rises in the east (if you didn't know – now would be a really, really good time to know this.) As the Sun rises, if you were to turn the right side of your body towards the Sun (remember Sun rises in east; your right side/arm would be east), north would be in front of you, south in back of you, and west on your left. So, if you knew that your destination was due west you would then turn your body towards the west and head in this direction. As the Sun moves (remember east to west) you can get a general idea of your direction by the Sun's movement.

"But what if it is nighttime?" you ask. If it is at night we would focus our attention to the North Star. But, before I go any farther, I will tell you that I was one of those people who thought you looked for the brightest star in the sky at night and that was the North Star ... t'aint so. First, we need to find the Big Dipper, and no, I am not referring to the big dope working at the local ice-cream shop. This is not an easy thing to do so I would highly suggest if you are in the city that you get out away from the city lights so you can see what stars actually look like. Maybe even printout a little sky map so you can tell what you are looking for.

This is one of the easiest method I found to find the North Star (*easier* is subjective mind you.) With your sky map in hand find the Big Dipper (it looks like a big ladle), then follow the outer two stars (in the upper right top corner of the cup – opposite the handle. Extend an imaginary line from the corner stars across the sky to the next bright star. Stretch your arm out full-length and spread your fingers and the North Star is approximately as far away as your thumb is to your middle finger. It is also true north.

Now back to your body as the compass. As you are looking at the North Star, east would be to your right, west to your left and south behind you.

The North Star doesn't move (well just so I don't get lambasted, let's say its movement is so small it's not noticeable), the stars and constellations rotate around it.

Your watch can also be used during the day to tell what direction you are going ... that is if the watch has hands. Take your watch off and hold it in the palm of your hand. Move your arm so the hour hand points at the sun (usually the smaller of the hands) imagine a line that runs through the center of the watch to a spot that is halfway between the hour hand and 12 on the dial. That would be north and south. (North is top of watch – south is bottom – remember?) Pretty cool, huh?

You can also place a stick into the ground, pointing directly towards the North Star and if you don't move the stick, each night it will always be pointing to the North Star.

As you can see, there are a lot of creative ways to learn what direction you are heading. You can also use vegetation, streams and rivers, what I mentioned above were merely a couple of ways. I suggest you do a little exploring on your own and research other means. But whatever means you find, and learn, remember your body compass, like the North Star, will always stay the same.

What You Can Do To Prepare

Remember head/face north, feet/back south, right east, and left west. Repeat after me … Sun rises in the east, the Sun sets … on the beaches of California – that's west. Oh, and how 'bout digging out your dad's old Timex watch, the one with the hands and put in your emergency go-bag … you know the one that takes a lickin' and keeps on tickin'?! – Just sayin'.

Hey Brother, Can You Spare A Dime?
Bartering With Metals

I was watching a morning television show one day when a commercial came on (like that's something new, right?!) It was a car commercial and the announcer was asking the television audience to bring them broken or unused gold jewelry and they would appraise the gold to use as a down payment on a car?! Was this guy talking about bartering with gold? This was the first time I had actually heard of precious metals being used for anything other than collecting or wearing; and certainly never for buying a car! Sure, we've all heard of "gold collectors" but this was different. This was a commercial/consumer business, who usually dealt in cash and/or on finance-based transactions.

So, I wondered, is this the beginning of a future bartering system? Do these business owners know something we don't? Are they subtly beginning to accept something other than "legal kinder" (er ... fiat money)? Is the dollar beginning to lose its value right under our nose and we aren't even realizing it?

I have to admit, I am not very good with all this financial forecast and economic stuff. I just try to keep up as best I can. But this got me to thinking. I've read a lot about the need to have a stash of pre-1964 silver coins and gold for bartering should there be an economic collapse ... or in layman's terms, should the dollar lose its buying power, so how about a little silver coin lesson? (Groan)

Silver coins that are pre-1965 (made before 1965) like quarters, dimes, and half-dollars were all minted with 90% silver. After 1965, coins were a mixture of copper and nickel. And, the only nickels with any silver in them were from 1942 to 1945 (only 35% silver). They were called "War Nickels." Half dollars (fifty-cent pieces) were 90% silver until 1964; then dropped to 40% silver from 1965 to 1970, and then from 1971 on they are silver-plated copper.

The reason you need to know about all this coin stuff, is because, pre-1965 U.S. quarters, half dollars and dimes are 90% silver and considered precious metals! Yep! They actually have more value than their face value. Even some of the seasoned coin collectors are collecting these coins more for content value than for their historic value.

What You Can Do To Prepare

So, all that coinage in the dark abyss at the bottom of your purse, in that big piggy bank, under the cushions of the sofa or car seats, those coins could be your salvation in the future.

Start dumping all your handbags out on the bed or the floor, and start combing through all the coins for pre-1964 coins. When you find one or two, separate them and put them in a safe place – again think precious metals (or investment). Also, check any coins you receive in change back from any cash purchases. Any time you see silver coins, make a habit of checking it to see if they are 90% silver coins.

Another thought is to use paper money to get coins back in return. Remember it's the paper that will one day be useless – not the 90% silver coins! Just a heads up, more and more people are becoming aware of the value of these coins and they are disappearing fast.

Penny for your thought! – Just sayin'.

Notes:

❧ 13 ❧
The Government

Beyond the Redwood Trees:
The Bohemian Grove

Now I will admit my formative years were mostly taken up with visions of shoes, clothes, shiny things, shoes, make-up and, did I mention shoes? So, as my eyes began to open to what some refer to as the real world, I couldn't help but be a little ... ah ... shocked (okay, a lot shocked) at what I have read and seen. How could I have missed all this going on around me? There are things that are going on in our own backyard (the United States) that a lot of us haven't a clue about. One such example is what is called "The Bohemian Grove," sounds cool huh?

Let me say, there was a time when anything that had the word "club" attached to it had my name all over it. Unfortunately, the *Bohemian Grove*, whose members are known as "Bohos" or "Grovers," is a no-girls-allowed club of over 2000 influential big name world-power elitists; with a lengthy waiting list.

The club holds an annual meeting every July, and has since 1872, at the Bohemian Groves, a 2700 acre retreat in the Redwood forest. Now, this is not retreat camping as we know it, these 2000 rich and powerful guests; consisting of major military contractors, and representatives of oil companies, banks, utilities, and national media. They come to listen to policy speeches and leisure pursuits of the world's elite.

I wondered how a club like could be kept such a ... hum, secret? I mean they have this ritual, where they dress up in these red robes and burn an effigy, called the "Cremation of Care", before a 40 foot tall ... hang on ...

274

you'll love this … owl. *Bwahahaha!* I mean really, an owl? I would have picked a black panther or a stallion … but an owl? Can you imagine? "Oh, wise and powerful Moloch the Owl …" But then I guess it is fitting for the World's most powerful whose-who's. Get it? *"whoo-hoo-hoo"* … like an owl? (Okay it was funny at the time.)

For two-weeks these powerful men do their "networking," men representing the government, military, industrial, and financial sectors of our Country, most of whom make major policy decisions. Some of the many attendees of these "July retreats" include the likes of every Republican president since Calvin Coolidge; former cabinet members Colin Powell, George Schultz and Henry Kissinger; former House Speaker Newt Gingrich; Dow Chemical Chairman, Frank Popoff and industrialist Stephen David Bechtel, Leonard Firestone, and David Rockefeller. They present and/or listen to speeches; known as "Lakeside Talks", containing information not available to *the outside.*

And get this, just like the tribes on the reality television show, *Survivor,* these guys have funny group/camp names too, like, Hill Billies, Mandalay, Cave Man, Stowaway, Uplifters, Owls Nest, Hideaway and Isle of Aves, Lost Angels, Silverado Squatters, Sempervirens, and Hillside - to name a few.

What You Can Do To Prepare

So what is the big deal about this secret annual July gathering? Well for me, it is that our Country's leaders and powerhouses are meeting with world leaders … in secret? – Just sayin'.

Ask Not What Your Country Can Do For You: Ask What You Can Do For Yourself

Okay, now this has always amazed me, and frankly, we've seen it over and over after a disaster has struck. That is, people waiting to be rescued, helped, or aided by the government. Just look at what happened with the *Hurricane Katrina* disaster – remember the natural disaster that became a man-made disaster. I know, I know, I seem to use *Hurricane Katrina* as an example a lot, but geeze, who hasn't seen all that devastation from the media coverage or in a magazine? People with misplaced logic carrying stolen items over their heads while wading in chest deep water, hordes in mass exodus trudging down the interstate with whatever they could muster to bring with them, people sitting on their roof tops waving frantically at the overhead helicopters, crowds hunkered on cots shoulder-to-shoulder, all visions that we can recall instantly.

After a disaster, there are going to be hours, days, and weeks before we might see assistance - and in some instances – not at all. People forget there is a chain of command; whether it is local, state, or federal governments. What I mean is everyone has a boss that they have to answer to before an action can take place – so if they are not given a command they are not going to respond. Sometimes it's not the government's fault for the delay in aid, but due to some overzealous citizens who start taking matters into their own hands with a "what's mine is mine and what's yours is mine too" attitude, thereby taking attention of the first responders away from the people in real need of assistance.

Disasters are not pretty. There are so many variables in what could happen and the delays that are created by these variables. Let's take the Katrina disaster again. Some residence of Louisiana knew the storm was coming, right? They knew it was a whopper of a hurricane, right? But some chose to stay put, and wait it out - resting on their laurels. After all, they had weathered storms in the past.

The government also knew it might be bad, but no one had ever experienced a disaster of *Hurricane Katrina's* size and magnitude so they didn't realize just how bad the storm would be.

The problem with resting on your laurels is that at some point and time you are going to have to get off those laurels (what a laurel anyhow?) ... okay ... and be accountable for your actions, either by your own doing or by the forces of nature.

What You Can Do To Prepare

So what is the point in all of this? The point is the government may not come to help you; or be able to come to your aide in time of a disaster. Think about it, if just some of us would prepare ourselves, imagine how much pressure could be taken off the first responders. Water lines, food lines, first-aid, these could all be minimized by us having our own supplies

Sure, there will come a time when our supplies will run out. But in the initial panic we can avoid being one of the hundreds, maybe thousands standing in line simply to get a bottle of water.

The government recommends that you have three days' worth of food and water for you and your family (72 hours)

... that's 72 hours. But realistically, you might want to plan on more like three weeks to three months of supplies for a major disaster

Learn to minimize your lifestyle now so it isn't such a shock when things turn bad. For those who are used to dining out for your meals or pushing the vending machine buttons every time your little tummy pinches, you are going to suffer the most. Instant gratification and disasters do not mix. Start with small steps like preparing soup and homemade sandwiches to eat at work and at home instead of going out to eat.

If you survive a disaster physically unscathed, count yourself blessed. It just doesn't seem fair that the injured should have to wait while a first responder tends to your need for a drink of water, when you knew to plan and prepare a head of time.

Oh, and if you really want a character strengthener try eating some of those weenies in a can. – Just sayin'.

NOTES

Only the Shadow Knows!
The Shadow Government and the Government's COG Plan

I watched a documentary of sorts called *"Day after Disaster"* on the History Channel. It was different from most apocalyptic and post-apocalyptic shows that we usually see on television. The documentary featured narratives and opinions by past and present government officials and experts who talked openly about their preparations should a catastrophic disaster strike the United States. It was based on a *"what if"* scenario of a nuclear bomb striking Washington D.C. What an eye opener!

Other than discussing the "woulda, shoulda, coulda's" of the nuclear strike itself … it also detailed the procedures set forth to secure our government in the face of the disaster. The government has a plan known as the Continuity of Government Plan (otherwise known as COG). The Continuity of Government Plan is devised to allow the government to continue operations in the event of a catastrophic disaster.

The COG plan was initially adopted in the United States during the Eisenhower administration, but was not utilized until the 9/11 terrorist attacks.

Not only will the president, vice-president, and on down the line of succession be whisked away to secured hiding places but also a group known as the *Shadow Government.*

Well let me tell you, this information intrigued the heck outta me, so I decided to do a little digging. What I found was that the Shadow Government could be placed in any number of mountainous underground security bunkers should something fatal happen to the president and vice-president.

The Shadow Government has anywhere from 75 to 150 (non-elected) senior civilian managers (depending on the number needed in a particular situation) who will live and work in bunkers on a rotating basis (or permanently, or until the country is back-up and running) to ensure the continuity of national security.

Another thing that was intriguing, are the bunkers themselves. The government has survival bunkers placed within a 300 mile radius of Washington D.C., so that at the drop-of-a-hat the appointed will be swiftly transported to safety. Some of the known bunkers sites (yes there are still those top-secret areas we don't know about) are as follows; Site R (also known as Raven Rock) a bunker in (yes I said in) a Pennsylvania mountain, and can accommodate 3,000 people. *Mount Weather* near Berryville, VA, is also built into a mountain and has a hospital, crematorium, emergency power plant, and sleeping cots for 2,000 people. And then, the decommissioned bunkers at the *Greenbrier* resort (under the resort) in West Virginia and at Mount Pony in Culpeper, VA.

The sobering thought from watching *"Day after Disaster"* is that our government is preparing for any number of disasters by having fully functional bunkers for safe-housing.

What You Can Do To Prepare

So, my question is this, "If the Government is preparing and planning to hunker down, don't you think it is prudent that we do the same?"

The government also holds annual anti-terror drills using the "Continuity in Government" procedures; sending government representatives to dozens of the classified emergency facilities (bunkers) stretching from the Maryland and Virginia suburbs to the foothills of the Alleghenies (those are the ones we know about.)

The government is preparing for their survival. Don't you think it is time we focused on our survival as well? – Just sayin'.

NOTES

ABOUT THE AUTHOR

Jane is a former city girl who was clueless about what was going on around her; politics, the economy, the threat of terrorism, and ever-changing weather patterns; it was so much easier to stay in her own little cozy existence. That is, until the life-threatening assault by two gunmen, three back-to-back direct hit hurricanes, the plummeting value of her home, and a dwindling 401K. She soon began to realize that things were not as rosy as she had once thought. Through personal experiences, and trial-by-fire, she has now made her mission to educate the masses on disaster preparedness.

Jane has become a preparedness expert, homesteader, and public speaker, as well as the editor of *www.SurvivorJane.com* one of the highest rated preparedness information websites for women. She is the founder and creator of Twitter hashtag #PrepperTalk; the largest preparedness community on Twitter, used internationally by people from all over the world.

Jane was featured on the hit television reality show National Geographic Channel's *Doomsday Preppers* (Season Four), and in *NEWSWEEK Special Edition: Off-Grid* magazine. Her work has been featured on National Geographic Channel's *Doomsday Preppers' BlogTV*, *Prepper and Shooter Magazine*, *PREPARE Magazine* and many other national preparedness blogs and magazines.

When Jane is not writing or public speaking you will find her out on her homestead; tending to the animals, gardening, preserving food, and enjoying life with husband, Rick Austin.

Made in the USA
Coppell, TX
29 March 2022

75734136R00167